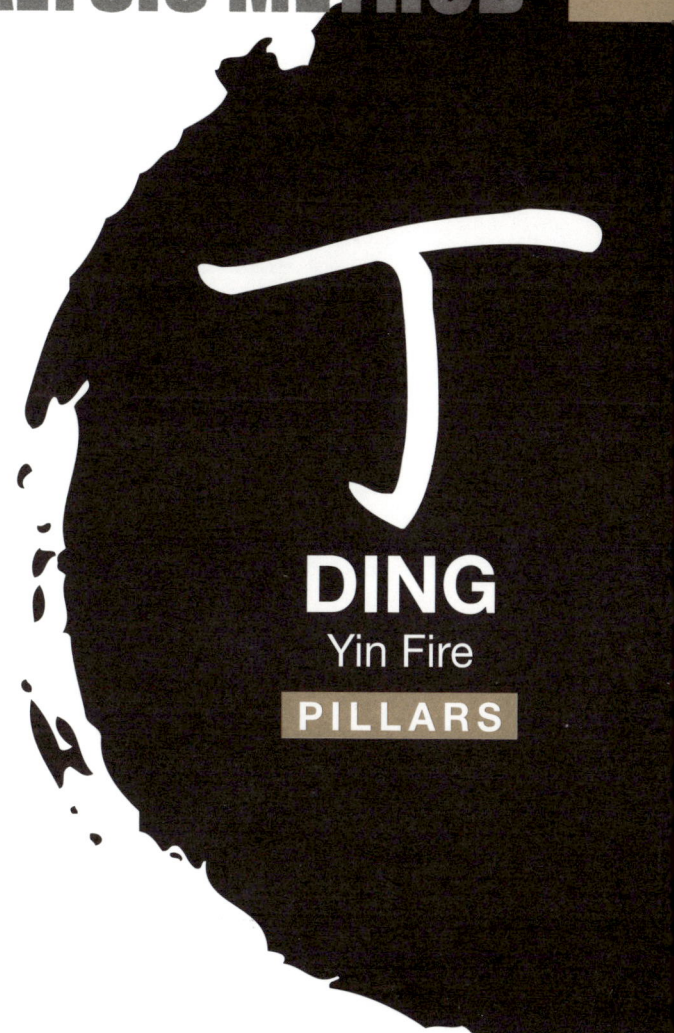

THE BAZI
60 PILLARS
LIFE ANALYSIS METHOD

一柱論命法

丁

DING
Yin Fire

PILLARS

The BaZi 60 Pillars Life Analysis Method - Ding Fire

Copyright © 2013 by Joey Yap
All rights reserved worldwide.
First Edition February 2013
Second Print August 2013

All intellectual property rights contained or in relation to this book belongs to Joey Yap.

No part of this book may be copied, used, subsumed, or exploited in fact, field of thought or general idea, by any other authors or persons, or be stored in a retrieval system, transmitted or reproduced in any way, including but not limited to digital copying and printing in any form whatsoever worldwide without the prior agreement and written permission of the author.

The author can be reached at:

Joey Yap Research International Sdn. Bhd. (939831- H)
19-3, The Boulevard, Mid Valley City,
59200 Kuala Lumpur, Malaysia.
Tel   : +603-2284 8080
Fax   : +603-2284 1218
Email   : info@masteryacademy.com
Website : www.masteryacademy.com

DISCLAIMER:

The author, Joey Yap and the publisher, JY Productions Sdn Bhd, have made their best efforts to produce this high quality, informative and helpful book. They have verified the technical accuracy of the information and contents of this book. Any information pertaining to the events, occurrences, dates and other details relating to the person or persons, dead or alive, and to the companies have been verified to the best of their abilities based on information obtained or extracted from various websites, newspaper clippings and other public media. However, they make no representation or warranties of any kind with regard to the contents of this book and accept no liability of any kind for any losses or damages caused or alleged to be caused directly or indirectly from using the information contained herein.

INDEX

1	**Introduction**	13
2	**Ding 丁 (Yin Fire)**	51
3	**DI TIAN SUI 滴天髓**	54
4	**Ding Fire According to Di Tian Sui 滴天髓**	55
5	**Ding Chou 丁丑 (Wood Ox)**	59
	• **Getting to Know Ding Chou 丁丑 (Fire Ox)**	61
	• **Work Life**	67
	• **Love and Relationships**	71
	• **Technical Analysis**	77
	• **Unique 60 Pillar Combinations**	83
	Heaven Combine Earth Punish 天合地刑 Ding Chou 丁丑 (Fire Ox) + Ren Xu 壬戌 (Water Dog)	84
	Heaven Combine Earth Harm 天合地害 Ding Chou 丁丑 (Fire Ox) + Ren Wu 壬午 (Water Horse)	86
	Heaven Friend Earth Clash 天比地沖 Ding Chou 丁丑 (Fire Ox) + Ding Wei 丁未 (Fire Goat)	88
	Heaven and Earth Clash 天沖地沖 Ding Chou 丁丑 (Fire Ox) + Gui Wei 癸未 (Water Goat)	90
	Heaven Counter Earth Clash 天尅地沖 Ding Chou 丁丑 (Fire Ox) + Xin Wei 辛未 (Metal Goat)	92
	Heaven and Earth Unity 天同地比 Ding Chou 丁丑 (Fire Ox) + Ding Chou 丁丑 (Fire Ox)	94
	Heaven and Earth Combo 天地相合 Ding Chou 丁丑 (Fire Ox) + Ren Zi 壬子 (Water Rat)	96
	Mutual Exchange Goat Blade 互換羊刃 Ding Chou 丁丑 (Fire Ox) + Gui Wei 癸未 (Water Goat)	98
	Rob Wealth Goat Blade 劫財羊刃 Ding Chou 丁丑 (Fire Ox) + Bing Wu 丙午 (Fire Horse)	99

6	**Ding Mao** 丁卯 (Fire Rabbit)	101
	• **Getting to Know Ding Mao** 丁卯 (Fire Rabbit)	103
	• **Work Life**	111
	• **Love and Relationships**	115
	• **Technical Analysis**	119
	• **Unique 60 Pillar Combinations**	125
	Heaven Combine Earth Punish 天合地刑 **Ding Mao** 丁卯 (Fire Rabbit) + **Ren Zi** 壬子 (Water Rat)	126
	Heaven Combine Earth Harm 天合地害 **Ding Mao** 丁卯 (Fire Rabbit) + **Ren Chen** 壬辰 (Water Dragon)	128
	Heaven Friend Earth Clash 天比地沖 **Ding Mao** 丁卯 (Fire Rabbit) + **Ding You** 丁酉 (Fire Rooster)	130
	Heaven and Earth Clash 天沖地沖 **Ding Mao** 丁卯 (Fire Rabbit) + **Gui You** 癸酉 (Water Rooster)	132
	Heaven Counter Earth Clash 天剋地沖 **Ding Mao** 丁卯 (Fire Rabbit) + **Xin You** 辛酉 (Metal Rooster)	134
	Heaven and Earth Unity 天同地比 **Ding Mao** 丁卯 (Fire Rabbit) + **Ding Mao** 丁卯 (Fire Rabbit)	136
	Heaven and Earth Combo 天地相合 **Ding Mao** 丁卯 (Fire Rabbit) + **Ren Xu** 壬戌 (Water Dog)	138
	Rob Wealth Goat Blade 劫財羊刃 **Ding Mao** 丁卯 (Fire Rabbit) + **Bing Wu** 丙午 (Earth Horse)	140

4　The BaZi 60 Pillars Life Analysis Method

7	**Ding Si 丁巳 (Fire Snake)**	143
	• **Getting to Know Ding Si** 丁巳(Fire Snake)	145
	• **Work Life**	153
	• **Love and Relationships**	157
	• **Technical Analysis**	163
	• **Unique 60 Pillar Combinations**	169
	Heaven Combine Earth Punish 天合地刑 **Ding Si** 丁巳 (Fire Snake) + **Ren Shen** 壬申 (Water Monkey)	170
	Heaven Combine Earth Harm 天合地害 **Ding Si** 丁巳 (Fire Snake) + **Ren Yin** 壬寅 (Water Tiger)	172
	Heaven Friend Earth Clash 天比地沖 **Ding Si** 丁巳 (Fire Snake) + **Ding Hai** 丁亥 (Fire Pig)	174
	Heaven and Earth Clash 天沖地沖 **Ding Si** 丁巳 (Fire Snake) + **Gui Hai** 癸亥 (Water Pig)	176
	Heaven Counter Earth Clash 天剋地沖 **Ding Si** 丁巳 (Fire Snake) + **Xin Hai** 辛亥 (Metal Pig)	178
	Heaven and Earth Unity 天同地比 **Ding Si** 丁巳 (Fire Snake) + **Ding Si** 丁巳 (Fire Snake)	180
	Heaven and Earth Combo 天地相合 **Ding Si** 丁巳 (Fire Snake) + **Ren Shen** 壬申 (Water Tiger)	182
	Rob Wealth Goat Blade 劫財羊刃 **Ding Si** 丁巳 (Fire Snake) + **Bing Wu** 丙午 (Fire Horse)	184

8	**Ding Wei 丁未 (Fire Goat)**	187
	• Getting to Know Ding Wei 丁未 (Fire Goat)	189
	• Work Life	197
	• Love and Relationships	203
	• Technical Analysis	207
	• Unique 60 Pillar Combinations	213
	Heaven Combine Earth Punish 天合地刑 Ding Wei 丁未 (Fire Goat) + Ren Xu 壬戌 (Water Dog)	214
	Heaven Combine Earth Harm 天合地害 Ding Wei 丁未 (Fire Goat) + Ren Zi 壬子 (Water Rat)	216
	Heaven Friend Earth Clash 天比地沖 Ding Wei 丁未 (Fire Goat) + Ding Chou 丁丑 (Fire Ox)	218
	Heaven and Earth Clash 天沖地沖 Ding Wei 丁未 (Fire Goat) + Gui Chou 癸丑 (Water Ox)	220
	Heaven Counter Earth Clash 天剋地沖 Ding Wei 丁未 (Fire Goat) + Xin Chou 辛丑 (Metal Ox)	222
	Heaven and Earth Unity 天同地比 Ding Wei 丁未 (Fire Goat) + Ding Wei 丁未 (Fire Goat)	224
	Heaven and Earth Combo 天地相合 Ding Wei 丁未 (Fire Goat) + Ren Wu 壬午 (Water Horse)	226
	Rob Wealth Goat Blade 劫財羊刃 Ding Wei 丁未 (Fire Goat) + Bing Wu 丙午 (Fire Horse)	228

9	**Ding You** 丁酉 (Fire Rooster)	231
	• **Getting to Know Ding You** 丁酉 (Fire Rooster)	233
	• **Work Life**	239
	• **Love and Relationships**	243
	• **Technical Analysis**	247
	• **Unique 60 Pillar Combinations**	255
	Heaven Combine Earth Harm 天合地害 Ding You 丁酉 (Fire Rooster) + Ren Xu 壬戌 (Water Dog)	256
	Heaven Friend Earth Clash 天比地冲 Ding You 丁酉 (Fire Rooster) + Ding Mao 丁卯 (Fire Rabbit)	258
	Heaven Friend Earth Punish 天比地刑 Ding You 丁酉 (Fire Rooster) + Ding You 丁酉 (Fire Rooster)	260
	Heaven and Earth Clash 天冲地冲 Ding You 丁酉 (Fire Rooster) + Gui Mao 癸卯 (Water Rabbit)	262
	Heaven Counter Earth Clash 天尅地冲 Ding You 丁酉 (Fire Rooster) + Xin Mao 辛卯 (Metal Rabbit)	264
	Heaven and Earth Unity 天同地比 Ding You 丁酉 (Fire Rooster) + Ding You 丁酉 (Fire Rooster)	266
	Heaven and Earth Combo 天地相合 Ding You 丁酉 (Fire Rooster) + Ren Chen 壬辰 (Water Dragon)	268
	Rob Wealth Goat Blade 劫財羊刃 Ding You 丁酉 (Fire Rooster) + Bing Wu 丙午 (Fire Horse)	270

八字一柱論命法

丁 Ding

10	**Ding Hai 丁亥 (Fire Pig)**	273
	• **Getting to Know Ding Hai 丁亥** (Fire Pig)	275
	• **Work Life**	281
	• **Love and Relationships**	285
	• **Technical Analysis**	289
	• **Unique 60 Pillar Combinations**	295
	Heaven Combine Earth Harm 天合地害 Ding Hai 丁亥 (Fire Pig) + Ren Shen 壬申 (Water Monkey)	296
	Heaven Friend Earth Clash 天比地沖 Ding Hai 丁亥 (Fire Pig) + Ding Si 丁巳 (Fire Snake)	298
	Heaven Friend Earth Punish 天比地刑 Ding Hai 丁亥 (Fire Pig) + Ding Hai 丁亥 (Fire Pig)	300
	Heaven and Earth Clash 天沖地沖 Ding Hai 丁亥 (Fire Pig) + Gui Si 癸巳 (Water Snake)	302
	Heaven Counter Earth Clash 天剋地沖 Ding Hai 丁亥 (Fire Pig) + Xin Si 辛巳 (Metal Snake)	304
	Heaven and Earth Unity 天同地比 Ding Hai 丁亥 (Fire Pig) + Ding Hai 丁亥 (Fire Pig)	306
	Heaven and Earth Combo 天地相合 Ding Hai 丁亥 (Fire Pig) + Ren Yin 壬寅 (Water Tiger)	308
	Rob Wealth Goat Blade 劫財羊刃 Ding Hai 丁亥 (Fire Pig) + Bing Wu 丙午 (Fire Horse)	310

Preface

In the past, even the most gifted BaZi students had a hard time getting to grips with the BaZi 60 Pillars. As some of my long time students may recall, the topic was originally covered in Module 4 of my BaZi Mastery program. I was often told that it would be wise to give the topic greater coverage and attention. When I upgraded the BaZi Mastery syllabus back in 2009, I decided that the best thing to do would be to cover the 60 Pillars exclusively in a *new* series of books – one of which you are reading now!

When I first began writing this series, I had no idea what I'd let myself in for. I had to call upon a lifetime of personal study and research, refer to classical interpretation and records and leverage all my years of BaZi Chart assessment and interpretation experience to get the job done. Most pressingly, because this book is intended for the average user of BaZi with little or no BaZi academic background, I had to condense and simplify my findings so that they would be easily understood. This, was hard.

I found the basic, technical elements of this writing process straight-forward. Accurately streamlining, condensing and translating the material from the original records took me a long time, however, and the greatest difficulty was to make sure that my translations and interpretations didn't deviate from or dilute the source material in any meaningful way.

I knew when writing this series that it was important to present the BaZi 60 Pillars in a practical way. This means I had to remove many of the rhetoric technical jargon. In the course of my work as a BaZi consultant, I've dealt with many leaders, businessmen, decision makers and visionaries as well as countless students and enthusiasts, too. One thing I have found in all my dealings is that people do not have the time to make use of the technical, classic-referencing BaZi information in the modern world. They want quick, accurate information which they can use to make decisions, motivate and influence others. Without some kind of intermediate system or technique, it simply takes too much time and experience to crack the Destiny Code and utilize its teachings. Business leaders in particular aren't interested in the technical details or academic history of BaZi. They don't have time to sit in a classroom - all they want is results!

To this end, I have created a unique format that allows anyone to utilize the BaZi 60 Pillars simply by plotting a chart and turning to the indicated page. I have condensed the original information found in the source texts and updated it with my own experience and findings for the modern world. I've already done all the hard, behind-the-scenes calculations and co-ordination for you. If you can look up information on a reference table and turn the page then you can leverage the full power of the BaZi 60 Pillars.

Creating this rapid delivery version of the 60 Pillars was difficult and time consuming but I know that my efforts will allow people all around the world to use the system for the first time with only a minimum of effort or pre-existing academic understanding. This makes it all worthwhile. The 60 Pillars Life Assessment method *used* to be a system known and understood only by the elite and those in academia – a system passed down in secret from generation to generation. I hope that this series of books finally brings the subject matter to the masses in a digestible, practical way.

I wish you the best of luck in your mission to master the BaZi 60 Pillars! If you wish to delve further into the subject matter after reading, then please do feel free to drop by my FaceBook (www.facebook.com/JoeyYapFB) or attend one of my workshops in the near future. I'll be thrilled to meet you.

Warmest regards,

Joey Yap
May 2013

Author's personal website : www.joeyyap.com

Academy websites : www.masteryacademy.com | www.baziprofiling.com

Joey Yap on Facebook : www.facebook.com/joeyyapFB

INTRODUCTION

INTRODUCTION

In many ways, life seems like a labyrinth which cannot be mapped or fully understood.

Many of us walk through life without a clear understanding of our impact on other people or the way things we do will impact ourselves. This lack of awareness can stunt our potential because we just don't know what we are doing, where we are going, or, if we know where we wish to go, how to get there.

Most commonly, people do not know what their purpose is. This stems from an inability to assess personal talents and abilities. The most successful people – the people who live up to the promise of their Destiny – live to their strengths. When someone has a clear picture of their strengths and weaknesses they would have a better shot at happiness and success. Furthermore, knowing what talents we possess helps us determine what we have the give to the world. The more we can give, the more value we possess in the eyes of those around us.

BaZi is something of a personal map for the labyrinth of life. It will help you to become the best possible version of you!

BaZi Astrology – The Map to Your Life

Your BaZi, or Destiny Code, describes your strengths and weaknesses. It can help you show you the maximum possible personal limits, based on what makes you, you. It dictates how far you can go in life, and what you can possibly achieve with the talent and potential you have been uniquely blessed with.

BaZi allows us to understand our Destiny and ultimately make better choices everyday. We can make a choice either to act upon life, rather than merely allowing life to act upon us.

Studying your BaZi Destiny Chart is similar to peeling an onion. There are many hidden layers of truth that you will uncover as you find out about yourself. By fully understanding your potential, you can both walk the shortest path to achievement and avoid dead ends in life that you are ill equipped to venture down.

BaZi can be used as a tool to:

A) Help us understand who we are.

- Understand our destiny
- Our character, personality, strengths, weaknesses
- Talents and abilities

B) Map of our life and Destiny.

- Events and circumstances that could benefit us
- Events and circumstances that could challenge us
- What lessons and insights we can gain from our experiences
- Help us grow
- Growth and progress leads us to happiness and fulfillment in life

When I speak of Destiny, it is easy to imagine that I mean a concrete series of life events over which you have no control. However, I believe that Destiny is not carved in stone. We all choose to either fulfill our Destiny or to ignore it and fail. Your BaZi chart can help you find your flow, allowing you to fulfill 100% of your potential.

All of us have distinctive talents and capabilities. Recognizing this and knowing exactly what these are can allow you to supercharge your progress and achieve far more than you ever thought possible during your lifetime.

Understanding your BaZi chart, which reveals these distinctive talents and capabilities, is therefore the key to unleashing your innate potential.

So, what are the limitations?

If BaZi is so powerful, why hasn't it helped every person in the world to become wildly successful? While this is certainly possible, one reason is that BaZi Astrology is a complicated affair. I've spent two decades of my life studying and teaching it.

To help make the subject more accessible, I've written five key books on BaZi. Together, they form the **Destiny Code** Series.

This collection of books serves as an introductory platform on BaZi for students, practitioners or teachers to heighten their knowledge and widen their skill.

Another reason that BaZi cannot truthfully guarantee wild riches and success in stone is because we simply cannot control everything that happens to us in life.

We are at the mercy of circumstance and changing fortunes. Going through life is like riding the waves of the ocean; events rush in one after another. Some circumstances, or events are trivial and cause little or no impact to our lives. While others can drastically change the playing field and knock us for six. Think family deaths, injuries and so on.

The good news for BaZi students is that even in the worst circumstances, BaZi allows us to gain control.

With BaZi we can learn what our options are. By understanding our options, we can make better choices – instead of drifting aimlessly down the river, we can choose which fork in the river we wish to travel down. This is the way in which we can all design our own Destiny, no matter what.

The Next Level: BaZi In 2013 And Beyond

It has long been my mission to bring the art and science of BaZi to the masses.

In the course of my BaZi consulting practice over the last seventeen years, I've met with many professionals, leaders of nations and heads of multinationals. I've worked closely with some of Asia's biggest CEOs– people whose lives are interesting and inspirational. These clients lead and inspire thousands of people.

When it comes to BaZi, these busy high achievers are not interested in 'studying the technicalities' – they demand quick methods and fast results. They only want a system which gives them the ability to make split second decisions based on a person's personality and potential (the key information imparted by BaZi, and the information which is of great value in the corporate world!)

Corporate clients simply don't need a FULL "Destiny reading". They are more interested in people development, people management and personality profiling.

They need a tool to help them influence and lead others better.

This realization led me to do further research into the system of BaZi in an attempt to simplify and streamline the system for instant 'personality assessment'. I made it my goal to update BaZi for the modern world.

To this end, I eventually created the "BaZi Profiling System" in order to help people kick start the process of learning about the source of their true perceptions and what they can do to shift their lives for the better without the need to understand the technical aspects of BaZi chart reading.

This lead me to another series of books focusing on personality profiling –which proved very popular among business professionals. For the first time, BaZi became widely accessible to everyone on Earth.

In my many years of BaZi teaching and writing, I have witnessed how the BaZi Profiling System helped thousands of people take control of their lives. Excitingly, the BaZi Personality Profiles are really just the beginning of the BaZi system, however.

What I offer you now is the next level of this profiling system. An advanced user level, if you may. Beyond BaZi Profiling is the traditional **Day Pillar analysis** – a method of reading I use whenever I do a career counseling with job seekers or corporate professionals. This technique is known as – the **60 Pillar Life Analysis** method, known in Chinese as "一柱論命法 Yi Zhu Lun Ming Fa."

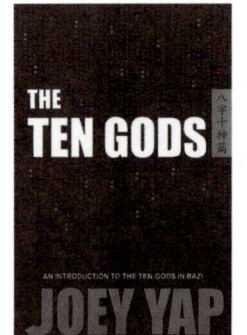

This book is intended for both the casual reader and professional practitioner. In this way, it has been written with the same mind set as one of my previous book on the Ten Stars of BaZi – **The Ten Gods**, which was a success with both of these demographics.

Before we go further, allow me to write a little about the history of BaZi so that you may have a base level of understanding before proceeding to... **A History to BaZi Methodologies.**

The current format of BaZi Astrology study was first introduced in the keystone reference of Zi Ping BaZi, by *XuZi Ping* 徐子平 (907-960), from the North region of the Song Dynasty 北宋. He was a famous author, with far-reaching knowledge in the field of Chinese Astrology that covered the Five Elements, the Ten Gods and various branches of the Chinese Metaphysical studies.

Later *Xu Le Wu* 徐樂吾 (1886 - 1949), a relatively recent scholar of BaZi, greatly contributed to the development of Zi Ping BaZi. His works include the ever-important 窮通寶鑑 *Qiong Tong Bao Jian* and 子平眞訣 *Zi Ping Zhen Jue* that served as an important reference point, especially in the Pictorial Method (an integral part of this book), for all serious BaZi practitioners.

Xu Le Wu's publications of these classics have since become the ideal point of reference in the field – his ideas borrowed, replicated, and reproduced by subsequent practitioners of his time and even up until the present day. Unfortunately, in my humble opinion, many of the modern day authors may have missed some of the important nuances in his original work - and have taken some of his meaning almost too literally.

Zi Ping Cui Yan 子平粹言 was perhaps *Xu Le Wu's* final book, and I believe the author wrote this book with hopes of teaching his students the correct way to use the Pictorial Method and incorporate a deeper understanding of the Five Element Theory.

The ancient texts from this 60 Pillar Life Analysis Method book are mainly derived from the classic reference of *Di Tian Shui* 滴天髓. According to the legend, *Di Tian Shui* is written by *Jing Tu* 京圖, the Yi Jing practitioner of the Song Dynasty. In the early Ming Dynasty, it was further explained and annotated by *Liu Cheng Yi* 劉誠意, who is also known as, the famous scholar - *Liu Bo Wen* 劉伯溫.

The ancient practitioners and teachers of BaZi always referred to the '*Di Tian Shui* 滴天髓 as one of the essential references because they believed the information in this book would bring clarity and complete understanding to the learners of this art, if they were able to unlock the meaning within the pages. However, this proved to be quite a challenging task as the classics were written in language that is filled with metaphors and obscure meanings. This has been overlooked by modern day authors who read it literally.

With that said, I applaud the effort of Mr. Hung Hin Cheong, one of the most accomplished students of mine and a successful engineer and corporate manager, in translating ancient passages of the *Di Tian Shui* and making the meaning clear and applicable to today's society. I've taken extracts from his excellent transliteration work and have included them in a section in this book.

Like *Xu Le Wu* 徐樂吾 (1886 - 1949), I realized today that there is a gap between the real science of BaZi and what was being offered or at least perceived in the mass market.

I also understand that another subtle problem facing BaZi today is the popularity of my very own Destiny Code series. I inadvertently created a breed of street-side practitioners who use my Destiny Code series of books. Of course, due to their lack of in-depth understanding of the concepts of the Five Elements and the Yin and Yang, some well-intended educators have merely taught their students the literal meaning of their readings; that is Jia being a big Tree and the Bing as the Sun. Serious practitioners known that the Pictorial Method drills far deeper than that. I hope this new book will help bring this notion to the general public and to the very same street-side practitioners!

At the end of it all, there are several ways to read a BaZi Chart. Each of these systems of analysis has its own benefits. By using these you will be able to look at a BaZi Chart from several different angles.

The Day Pillar Analysis

Using 60 Pillars Analysis in the BaZi system truly takes your BaZi reading to a deeper level. The most important part of the BaZi Chart for this purpose is the Day Pillar which contains the Day Master – an area of the BaZi Chart you will already be intimately familiar with after reading my BaZi Profiling or Destiny Code books.

The Day Pillar is perhaps the most important part of the BaZi Chart when it comes to discovering inner strength. Therefore, a more intricate understanding of the Day Pillar can allow you to greatly appreciate your talents and abilities. This insight can also help you learn how to become a better communicator, a better lover, a better friend, and find success in your life.

While I am a firm believer in positive thinking, I do not subscribe to the belief that we can simply 'psyche' ourselves into finding success or inner peace. I believe positivity is achieved when we are true to our nature. Our innate personality. By appreciating our born talents and capitalizing on them. By truly knowing who we are and becoming a better version of ourselves. I believe we can do this best through enhanced understanding of the BaZi 60 Day Pillars. Learning about the 60 Day Pillars is one way in which we can find our groove and begin climbing the mountain of progress – leading to fulfillment and happiness.

Advancing the Study of BaZi

Some of the more common, traditional ways of reading a BaZi Chart are as follows:

- The Strong Weak Analysis
- Useful God Analysis
- Auxiliary Stars
- Structural Analysis Method
- Five Elements Method
- Ten God Analysis Method
- Pictorial Method
- Na Yin Analysis Method
- Ascending and Descending Qi

My own practice of BaZi has grown over the years. Like any passionate student of BaZi, I first started out seeking revered BaZi masters for guidance and researched the ancient classics to uncover all the so called 'secrets' embedded directly or indirectly from the classics. I hoped to find things that had been lost in translation at the original source. Many 'devotees' (this is what I like to call the extremist researchers) keep digging into the past records and needless to say, most of them become what people would normally describe as the academic ivory towers.

I love the classics and I love pure research but I also like seeing the practical side of Chinese Metaphysics. I want to see it used and applied in the real world. I have found that BaZi has great utility in the business community where RESULTS are what count! (The fact my consulting firm continues to retain top corporate clients using BaZi Profiling in business is probably the best proof that it really does work wonders – if it didn't, we would have been shown the door long ago).

I've worked with the heads of businesses and leaders of nations and I can tell you for a fact – they are not interested in how well I can explain a theory or how well-versed I am in the history of BaZi. They want to know one, simple thing: how can I help them with their business. In other words, they say 'Show Me The Money'.

Over the years, I've come to realize that BaZi could be upgraded and re-packaged for the modern world. It could serve as the beating heart in a new, rapid deployment system for use in business and by people who want accurate results and answers without having to know how the system works or where it came from, necessarily. The 60 Pillars Life Analysis Method that I share with you in this book is an old method that I have brought firmly into the 21st century for today's practical world.

The methods presented here are based on *Xu Le Wu's* original Pictorial description of the Stems. I've taken the liberty to refine them and make the whole thing suitable for the modern audience.

As people continue to learn the BaZi and the tradition grows, there is no doubt in my mind that more of these old and new analysis methods will come forward.

The update and modification I've made also means that I have an additional method to share that is a total revolution to the modern BaZi system. This BaZi reading method is called the new Joey Yap's Pictorial Analysis Method and it is going to completely change the way that people learn BaZi. My goal is to present a comprehensive and wonderful system that is known as the BaZi, in a way that is more understandable and easily digested by the people who have a desire to learn its secrets.

The Pictorial Analysis Method is the next step in my passion project of bringing BaZi to everyone.

The Pictorial Analysis Method

The Pictorial Analysis Method I write of in this book is a shorthand that allows the reader to very quickly assess the 60 Pillars. It is one of the main methods I've used to deduce the meaning and attributes of each of the 60 Pillars. Now this does not mean this is the ONLY format, because we also take into consideration the Five Elements, the Ten Gods, the Twelve Growth and Birth Phases, the Auxiliary Stars and Na Yin components of each pillar. I've incorporated all these into some sort of a picture form for the pillar. Each of the 60 Pillars in this book has an associated picture. This concept relies heavily on the concept of Imagery or images, used as the backbone of Yi Jing (I-Ching), the book of changes, as well as a deep understanding of the Five Elements.

Why have I opted to use this picture-based system?

Learning the BaZi system in depth is a daunting task. This is why I created the BaZi 60 Pillars Analysis Method - in order to help make the system more understandable, palatable, and digestible from several different angles. Instead of reading and memorizing list after list of signs, elements, traits, and ideas, you can learn the BaZi system based off of images that represent the energy behind each of the 60 Pillars.

They do say that a picture paints a thousand words and I am a firm believer in the saying! Many history books as well as classic Chinese literature have used imagery to backup BaZi, just as I do here. In fact, the translations of the specific meanings of the words connected to the BaZi reveal that each sign are called by names that suitably relate to a very specific, defined image. For example:

- Jia 甲 Wood   – Big Tall Tree

- Yi 乙 Wood   – Flower

- Bing 丙 Fire   – Sunlight

- Ding 丁 Fire   – Candle

- Wu 戊 Earth   – Big Rock

- Ji 己 Earth   – Soft Earth

- Geng 庚 Metal   – Large Axe

- Xin 辛 Metal   – Fine Jewelry

- Ren 壬 Water   – Great Ocean

- Gui 癸 Water   – Misty Rain

The BaZi 60 Pillars Life Analysis Method

八字一柱論命法

Ding

I have taken these specific and detailed translations and transformed them into a new way of learning, reading, and getting to the heart of the BaZi. The reason my picture-based system works so well is simple – humans are very visual. It is much easier for us to recall an image than it is words, ideas, or phrases. We even think in picture form. When we are working something out in our minds, imagery will form to help us sort out our issues. Pictures and simple imagery help us make sense of our lives. This is why, in my opinion, the Pictorial Analysis Method is so effective. It allows me to directly convey the essence of the BaZi message through imagery. These images are much easier to remember than words.

There are a number of things that should be discussed before the reader begins to use the Pictorial Analysis Method. Mostly, I wish to address the idea that these pictures should NOT be taken completely literally.

Consider the ever popular BaZi 101 remedy: Jia Wood 甲 = A Big Tree. In the ancient classics, for Jia Wood, a 'metaphorical' description is used to describe the Jia. The original author in the ancient classics was trying to portray the Wood of Jia Wood as having similar attributes to a tree.

The tree spoken of here is just a metaphor. One needs to think further, using the imagery of a tree only as a starting point, to grab the real meaning behind the picture. What the author was really saying about Jia Wood is that it embodies the idea of 'growth' (like a tree), it is about production and progress, it is about the starting of a journey or a cycle, etc.

Regrettably, some of my own students who have ventured out to start their own school of BaZi without completing their studies seem to have only taken the 'literal meaning' of the Pictorial Method with them. Some go all out to say that Jia is represented by the Big Tree and if one wants to enhance the element of Jia Wood, he or she is advised to wear green, or plant big trees in their residence. This concept has been taken out of context and is certainly not in line with my teachings or the teachings of this book. I'll say it again: think metaphorically, not literally.

I want to educate students and those that are interested in learning BaZi the correct way to utilize the Pictorial Method - the way I intend to teach in my previous BaZi Module 4 program - and rectify the problem of literal interpretation in BaZi overall.

Further Learning

To complete your BaZi study and practice, you must first know that the Pictorial Method is a very complex subject. A simple class that expands on this topic can go on and on for days. The reason for this is simple: it is important! If you are serious about a solidifying your understanding of BaZi and the 60 Pillars Life Analysis Method in particular, then you need to go the distance. As such, I strongly encourage readers and practitioners to attend my learning programs and classes, to absorb knowledge beyond the pages, and to further their studies in an understandable and accurate manner with a qualified BaZi teacher or better yet, be your own teacher and invest time in studying the classics. Or perhaps, we can even meet in person in my yearly seminars so that I can exchange ideas with you on this wonderful subject called BaZi.

The Pictorial Method is not intended to be used in isolation.

Know that the Pictorial Method only gives a partial answer; it is but one part of the puzzle. The pictures do not necessarily correspond to a good or bad outcome. They are not meant to be taken at literal, face value – use them simply to get a gut feeling about the Pillar in question.

There is a danger that newer students will use the Pictorial Method as something of a crutch, ignoring the importance of the Five Elements in the process.

Remember, the pictures are to help you understand and interpret the meaning of the Pillar, and they do NOT replace the importance of the Five Elements or the Ten Gods in BaZi. BaZi is fundamentally a Five Element study, so bear this in mind. As such, Jia Wood, although a tree, is still fundamentally a WOOD element. It represents growth, progress, production and new beginnings. Though it may be painted as a big tree, it is still very much a WOOD element. Likewise, Bing Fire 丙 may be visualized as the bright and majestic sunlight Fire, but, in fact, this Pillar still belongs to the FIRE element.

Taking the method too literally may lead others to make the wrong assumption as pictorially Jia Wood (Tree) cannot produce the Bing Fire (Sun). This is where the over-simplification of Pictorial Method is evident, for it evokes possible misinterpretation. Jia, being Wood, can always produce Bing as it is Fire. Wood will always produce Fire. The condition, however, needs to be considered. If the Wood is Wet, then producing Fire is difficult. However if the Wood is Dry, the Fire will be produced. You can judge this from looking at the Season or the surrounding elements. The pictures, in this case, help you visualize this.

One also needs to understand that to facilitate their BaZi knowledge, they need to incorporate the knowledge of the Five Elements, the Ten Gods, and the Twelve Growth Phrases, information that I have incorporated in the BaZi 60 Pillars Life Analysis Method series to provide a more comprehensive learning experience to students.

To The Critics

Of course, with a new way of doing things comes criticism. My attempts to expand the ancient teachings with this new system have not gone uncriticized. I accept this and I would even say I expected it! With any breakthrough system, there is going to be a certain amount of criticism. Great masters of the past like *Xu Zi Ping* 徐子平, *Li Xu Zhong* 李虛中, *Xu Le Wu* 徐樂吾, *Ren Tie Qiao* 任鐵橋, *Yuan Shu Shan* 袁樹珊 and *Wei Qian Li* 韋千里 were heavily criticized during their time. Their work is now accepted as ground breaking and progressive. I welcome criticism because I know and I trust that this expansion of the BaZi is going to help this system of Astrology thrive and help people to improve their lives. However, as I tell my students: There are no statues in this world that are erected in honor of a critic.

The BaZi 60 Pillars

What are the BaZi 60 Pillars?

There are 60 possible combinations of the Five Elements and their different polarities which make up the 60 Pillars. Each Pillar has its own Element and in this book you will find that each of these Pillars has its own pictorial representation, too. By seeing these images you will be able to remember the energies that are connected to the different Elements more easily. When you look at the image for each pillar you remember the name and energy behind that pillar. For example, instead of calling it a Wood Rat or a Wood Horse, you will see an image of the energy that equates to Wood Rat or Wood Horse.

Each book in the BaZi 60 Pillars series deals with one of the ten possible Day Masters. As such, one doesn't need to read all the 10 books in the series; only the one associated with his or her Pillar. Each one of the books is largely written with the Day Pillar in mind.

For the Month, the Year, or the Hour Pillar, readers need to make some minor adjustments on their own in order to derive meaning suitable for the reading represented by each Pillar.

These Pillars are made up of the Ten Stems and the Twelve Branches. Each of the Pillars has one Heavenly Stem and one Earthly Branch.

The Heavenly Stem

The Heavenly Stem is known as the prevailing Qi or surface Qi, located at the top of the Pillar. This refers to the external, publicly visible personality and traits of a person. Here we learn about the personality, traits, and outlook that an individual shows to the world. It is the characteristic, personality or outlook that your friends, family, acquaintances know.

There are ten Heavenly Stems in total; they are made up of the Yin and Yang polarities of the Five Elements:

- Jia 甲 (Yang) Wood
- Yi 乙 (Yin) Wood
- Bing 丙 (Yang) Fire
- Ding 丁 (Yin) Fire
- Wu 戊 (Yang) Earth
- Ji 己 (Yin) Earth
- Geng 庚 (Yang) Metal
- Xin 辛 (Yin) Metal
- Ren 壬 (Yang) Water
- Gui 癸 (Yin) Water

Earthly Branch

The Earthly Branch is the bottom of the Pillar. Think of the hidden roots of a tree. It is the foundation – where your Pillar rests - and therefore, it represents the foundation of who you are.

The Earthly Branch carries the Qi and is considered a stronger influence on an individual's life than the Heavenly Stem is, albeit one which is hidden to others. When we assess the Earthly Branch, we can get a glimpse into the real, secret and hidden attitudes and nature of a person.

The Earthly Branch plays an important role in BaZi analysis as it not only carry the force of time but also represent the seasons and tells us about the strengths of the elements in the Chart.

The Palaces

In the BaZi system the Earthly Branches are made up of Four Pillars. Each of the Pillars signifies a different aspect of your life. The Day Pillar is the most significant because it is made up of both the Heavenly Stem and the Earthly Branch and it is determined by your date of birth, also known as your Day Master.

The Four Pillars

- Hour
- Day
- Month
- Year

時 Hour	日 Day	月 Month	年 Year	
				天干 Heavenly Stems
				地支 Earthly Branches
				藏干 Hidden Stems

The Hour Pillar

This is the Pillar that is connected to your ambitions, hopes and dreams. This is the Pillar of inspiration and your inner personality. The Hour Pillar can also tell us about life in old age as well as relationships with children and subordinates.

Hour Pillar Breakdown	
Conventional View	- Heavenly Stem and Earthly Branch : Children
Life Path	- Heavenly Stem and Earthly Branch : Old Age
Family Relation	- Heavenly Stem: Son - Earthly Branch: Daughter
Psychological Makeup	- Earthly Branch: Entertainment and treatment of subordinates
Psychological View	- Heavenly Stem: Passion - Earthly Branch: Desire

丁 Ding

八字一柱論命法

時 Hour | 日 Day | 月 Month | 年 Year

天干 Heavenly Stems
地支 Earthly Branches
藏干 Hidden Stems

The Day Pillar

This is the Pillar that is determined by the Day Master. It is connected to your inner spirit and your soul. This reveals the way that you communicate with others and the world around you. It also describes physical health. Finally, the Day Pillar is representative of your connection with your spouse.

Hour Pillar Breakdown	
Conventional View	- Heavenly Stem: Self - Earthly Branch: Spouse
Life Path	- Heavenly Stem and Earthly Branch : Mid Age
Family Relation	- Heavenly Stem: Self - Earthly Branch: Spouse
Psychological Makeup	- Heavenly Stem: Inner Spirit - Earthly Branch: Affinity
Psychological View	- Heavenly Stem: Personal view of life - Earthly Branch: Physical body

The Month Pillar

This Pillar is connected to your ambitions. It will also offer insight on your character and your upbringing. It is also connected to the way you handle responsibility and your self control. It can also show you the effect your parents have had and continue to have upon your life. Finally, this Pillar governs your likely career success and/or your business achievements.

Month Pillar Breakdown	
Conventional View	- Heavenly Stem and Earthly Branch: Parents
Life Path	- Heavenly Stem and Earthly Branch: Youth
Family Relation	- Heavenly Stem: Father - Earthly Branch: Mother
Psychological Makeup	- Earthly Branch: Responsibility and self control
Psychological View	- Heavenly Stem: Ambition - Earthly Branch: Character and upbringing

The Year Pillar

This is the Pillar that is connected to your overall gratitude for life. It can describe your morals and ethical integrity. It also describes the way you handle the important matters in your life. The Year Pillar is the cornerstone of your approach to family. It is connected to your relationships with your grandparents and your ancestors. In a modern context, The Year Pillar also represents one's social status and chosen circle of friends.

Year Pillar Breakdown	
Conventional View	- Heavenly Stem and Earthly Branch: Grandparents
Life Path	- Heavenly Stem and Earthly Branch: Childhood
Family Relation	- Heavenly Stem: Ancestor Home - Earthly Branch: Ancestor Tomb
Psychological Makeup	- Earthly Branch: Way of handling matters
Psychological View	- Heavenly Stem: Health - Earthly Branch: Gratitude, morals, and family

時 Hour	日 Day	月 Month	年 Year	
				天干 Heavenly Stems
				地支 Earthly Branches
				藏干 Hidden Stems

八字一柱論命法

丁 Ding

The Hour Pillar and the Day Pillar are both connected to the internal side of your personality. These two Pillars represent your inner self that you keep hidden from others. Interestingly, these are the parts of yourself that you might not even be aware of. See if what you read rings true!

The Applications

As the BaZi 60 Pillars series is written in the context of the Day Pillar, some adjustments are needed in the event where the Month, Year or the Hour Pillar is read.

Before you begin your learning, you need to find out your own Day Pillar, by plotting out your personal BaZi chart (Go to **www.joeyyap.com/bzchart**). Look at the Day Pillar and find the correct book in the series that matches it. For instance, if your Day Pillar is Gui Wei 癸未, you will need to study the Gui 癸 (Yin Water) Pillar book. Similarly, look for the Ding 丁 (Yin Fire) Pillar book if Ding Hai 丁亥 is your Day Pillar.

時 Hour	日 Day	月 Month	年 Year	
	癸 Gui Yin Water (DM)			天干 Heavenly Stems
	未 Wei Goat Yin Earth (Grave)			地支 Earthly Branches
	乙 Yi -Wood 食EG 己 Ji -Earth 殺7K 丁 Ding -Fire 才IW			藏干 Hidden Stems

The BaZi Chart above indicates that the Day Pillar is Gui Wei 癸未. Therefore, refer to the Gui 癸 (Yin Water) Pillar book to read the Pillar's analysis.

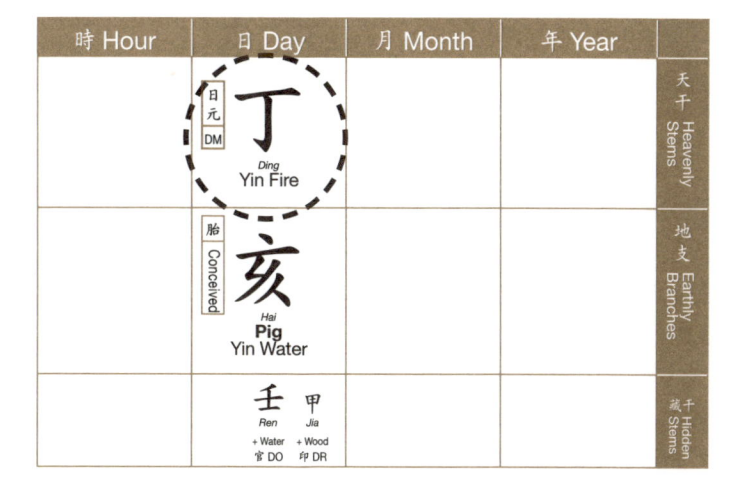

時 Hour	日 Day	月 Month	年 Year	
	丁 *Ding* Yin Fire (DM)			天干 Heavenly Stems
	亥 *Hai* Pig Yin Water (Conceived)			地支 Earthly Branches
	壬 *Ren* + Water 官 DO / 甲 *Jia* + Wood 印 DR			藏干 Hidden Stems

丁 Ding

八字一柱論命法

The BaZi Chart above indicates that the Day Pillar is Ding Hai 丁亥. Therefore, refer to the Ding 丁 (Yin Fire) Pillar book to read the Pillar's analysis.

In this method, the Day Pillar is read as the primary Pillar of your life. It is placed up in front in the foreground with the most power, control, and influence in your life.

The remaining three Pillars; the Year Pillar, the Month Pillar, and the Hour Pillar, are all in the background. They will affect, support, and change the energy of the Day Pillar. Learning to understand the interaction between the foreground and the background will tremendously enhance the effectiveness of your readings.

The Format of this Book

There are five sections in each individual Pillar. This breakdown of information allows for systematic learning.

The subject of Chinese Metaphysics was founded on the principles of Yi Jing, based on the concept of Qi 氣 (Five Elements), Numerology 數 (methods, methodology, formulae), and Images 像 (The essence of the Pictorial Method). While the Pictorial Method references the third technique (Images), it shouldn't be applied or studied in a manner that is mutually exclusive of the other two.

Therefore these books are written to include these two aspects. At the same time, however, there's a dilemma that if I make the book too technical, students would have a hard time comprehending the information due to the lack of groundwork.

To make the information more accessible, I divided the book into five sections for each Pillar. The first section is written in layman style, with very basic character analysis and personality assessment. The second section and beyond drill in on the technical analysis and reveals some of the working behind the 60 Pillars, hopefully to pique your interest in furthering your study by researching on the more notable ancient classics such as *Qiong Tong Bao Jian* 窮通寶鑒, *Zi Ping Zhen Quan* 子平眞詮, *Di Tian Sui* 滴天髓, *Zi Ping Zhen Jue* 子平眞訣, *Zi Ping Jing Cui* 子平精粹.

> **Before Each Chapter**

Several images that embody the many possible representations of the Pillar are presented in this section. This serves as a pictorial guide to help you better visualize each Pillar as you study.

> **1 First Section**
> **General descriptions of the Stems**
> **(For all the Stems in a Pillar).**

This part gives an overview of each Stem, and provides you with a general impression before you delve deeper into the following sections.

> **2 Second Section**
> **Classic Extraction from Di Tian Shui 滴天髓**

This section is extracted from the works by Mr. Hung Hin Cheong, who spent countless hours translating the ancient texts of Di Tian Sui. The classical texts of Di Tian Sui provide a solid platform for any learner of BaZi of any experience level to begin and advance their knowledge in the field. The book of Di Tian Sui can be divided into two chapters: Tong Shen Lun 通神論' (The Theosophy) and Liu Qin Lun 六親論 (The Six Relations).

As a side note, in my opinion any serious students of BaZi should try to study and unlock the information in the Di Tian Sui on their own or with a qualified teacher. It is after all, the book of foundation in BaZi study.

Third Section
General Observation of the Pillar

Matters of marriage, career, wealth and family are expanded upon in this section. This section is mercifully written in a simple way, free from jargon and technical lingo. You can also look at the section on Famous Personalities where notable people with similar Day Pillar are listed. These famous case studies help better illustrate the information given.

Fourth Section
Technical Analysis

This section contains some technical aspects pertaining to this BaZi Pillar. It is necessary to have some prior knowledge on BaZi to fully grasp the content in this section.

Fifth Section
The 60 Pillars Unique Combination

Assess the likely outcome of different Pillars combinations; good or bad. You can also learn the specific structure name and advance your skills by understanding the analysis behind each combination.

DO THIS FIRST

Print your BaZi Chart to facilitate your learning process as you use this book.

To plot your BaZi Chart:

www.masteryacademy.com/regbook

Here is your unique code to access the BaZi Calculator:

QLM0627

丁
Ding

八字一柱論命法

八字一柱論命法

丁 Ding

The following steps will guide you to plot your BaZi Chart with ease.

Step 1: Upon access to the site, key in the required information - Name, Gender, Hour, Day, Month and Year of Birth - as per instruction.

Step 2: Your BaZi Chart will be generated accordingly. (A sample is illustrated below.)

Step 3: Print your BaZi Chart.

Step 4: Begin CHAPTER 1.

Sample: This is how your BaZi Chart will look like

50 The BaZi 60 Pillars Life Analysis Method

丁
DING
Yin Fire
PILLARS

Ding 丁 (Yin Fire)

When we hear that someone has a Fire-based Day Master is may be easy to imagine them as having a fierce, fiery temper. Contrary to this, Ding 丁 Fire people are actually gentle, fun and easygoing souls. Think of a candle flame, emanating brightness and warmth – not a blazing fire.

Ding Fire individuals are warm, personable and sophisticated enough to think about how their decisions affect others. They would never dream of doing something to make another person unhappy or uncomfortable. They are lighting quick decision makers. In most situations, this makes them highly effective, where hang wringing might lead to missed opportunity. They are also thorough to a fault. Intellectual by nature, Ding Fire's love to learn more and need to know all there is to know before they develop confidence. They demand evidence before they believe something. They are close to their family, and tend to be loving and generous.

If you do manage to get on the wrong side of a Ding Fire person, you will wish you hadn't. Their temper, once unleashed, is fierce. Sometimes Ding Fire individuals can seem inconsistent or mercurial to deal with. If they are smiling in the morning they might not be by lunch time. This is because they have a thin skin and are easily upset or angered. Sometimes this leads to those around them feeling like they have to walk on eggshells. Although they are quick at making decisions, accuracy is sometimes compromised as a result. Because they don't usually sit down to weigh up the options, Ding Fires can make foolish, impulsive choices on occasion.

DI TIAN SUI 滴天髓

The Classic Text

Introduction

The information presented in this book comes from the original source, the famous classical text on BaZi called Di Tian Sui 滴天髓.

Di Tian Sui 滴天髓 can be credited as one of the important works of Liu Bo Wen 劉伯溫, a renowned military strategist, statesman and metaphysics scholar in the late Yuan and early Ming period of the 14th century. Liu Bo Wen was highly regarded for his contributions in the study of astronomy, Feng Shui as well as philosophy.

Liu Bo Wen was also a poet, and when he composed the original Di Tian Sui texts, he wrote it as a poem. Thus, the language used was so cryptic that scholars over the decades continue to find it a challenge to decipher the poem's true meaning.

In the following pages, you will find the original text on Ding Fire as written by Liu Bo Wen and its interpretation and transliteration extracted from Mr Hung Hin Cheong. Mr Hung has also contributed his commentary on the original texts in this book.

Ding Fire According to Di Tian Sui 滴天髓

Original Text by Liu Bo Wen

> 丁火柔中，內性昭融，
> 抱乙而孝，合壬而忠，
> 旺而不烈，衰而不窮，
> 如有嫡母，可秋可冬。

Interpretation by Hung Hin Cheong

Ding Fire is soft (yielding) at the core, having an accommodating nature. Filial when embracing Yi, loyal when combined with Ren. Prosperous but not fierce, weak but not exhausted. Will endure Autumn and Winter in the presence of its mother.

Commentary by Hung Hin Cheong:

Ding (丁) Fire is synonymous with Li (离) Fire, internally yin and externally Yang, hence the descriptions "yielding at the core" and "accommodating nature".

Yi (乙) is mother to Ding. Ding protects Yi so that Yi is not harmed by Xin (辛) Metal, unlike Bing's (丙) tendency to burn Jia (甲) Wood.

Ren (壬) is husband to Ding. Ren water fears Wu (戊) earth, but ding combines with Ren so that it cannot be harmed by Wu. This is unlike Ji (己) earth combing with Jia (甲) (to produce earth), and Xin (辛) metal combining with Bing (丙) (to produce water), whereby the combinations cause Jia and Bing to change their nature. [This argument is hard to conceptualize. Better to say Ding combines with Ren to produce Wood, which then controls Wu Earth to lessen its power; or water is vaporized by fire thus escaping control by earth.]

When in season, Ding Fire prospers, but does not overheat. Out of season it weakens but does not extinguish. (Fires dies at You (酉) but Ding is born at You.)

If Jia or Yi appears in the Stems, ding born in Autumn is unafraid of metal. If Yin (寅) or Mao (卯) appears in the Branches, Ding born in Winter does not fear water.

[Joey Yap: Time of birth is critical for Ding Fire. Only daytime Ding Fire (fire of the cauldron) is able to melt metal, but ding is outshone by Bing in the daylight hours. Ding Fire at night (candle light) is visible but cannot melt metal. Hence the best time of birth for Ding is You, when the sun sets and ding becomes visible, and the ding fire is still able to melt metal.]

丁丑

Ding Chou

丁丑 Ding Chou | 丁卯 Ding Mao | 丁巳 Ding Si | 丁未 Ding Wei | 丁酉 Ding You | 丁亥 Ding Hai

Getting to Know

Ding Chou 丁丑 (Fire Ox)

丁丑

Ding Chou

Positive Imagery

丁丑 Fire Ox

八字一柱論命法

Negative Imagery

八字一柱論命法

丁丑

Fire Ox

Getting to Know
Ding Chou 丁丑 (Fire Ox)

General Observations:

Ding Chou individuals are welcoming, friendly and kind. Often thought of as idealists, they are known to be sensitive and intellectual. There are two very important traits that will serve them well throughout their lives: strong-will and original thinking. This means that their ingenious determination will produce highly successful results.

Privileged with being both wise and astute, they will work diligently on a project or cause that they feel passionately about. They are naturally intuitive and possess a budding spirituality that enables them to assess the meaning of situations almost immediately. With proper nurturing, their spirituality will blossom to its full potential.

Staying ahead of progressive trends is highly important to the Ding Chou. Their imaginative mind always drives them in search of new and exciting ventures. These ventures help them to keep active and busy.

The Ding Chou is also inherently endowed with a sense of justice and compassion. They possess strong convictions and will use these traits to fight for their rights and the rights of others. They are likely to veer towards activism for a cause or movement they support.

These individuals are very prosperous in their early years. Once they are on a streak of good fortune, they do not give it up. The key to success for them is to maintain a positive singular focus. Also, in order to reach that level of success and prosperity, they must be persistent, tenacious and patient. They tend to continue to experience prosperity well into their later years, even more so than when they were younger.

Learning how to allow life unfold on its own is an important lesson for the Ding Chou. Once mastered, they will be able to stay in touch with their own sensitivity as well as enjoy spontaneity in life instead of trying to take control of every detail. They will only gain this inner knowledge and ability through self-analysis and regular periods of meditation.

The Ding Chou has a natural talent for arts and craft. They are intellectually inquisitive and have a healthy craving for knowledge and wisdom. They love to seek answers to the mysteries of life and hence their interest in the studies of psychology, natural universal laws, metaphysical art or even, the paranormal.

Individuals of Ding Chou are also gifted with a natural inclination for the field of gastronomy, with a particular focus on gourmet cuisine. They love food and would sniff out the most exquisite culinary delights, and are always on the lookout for the newest destination in dining excellence. Don't be surprised to find the Ding Chou excelling in the art and science of cooking, as they have the making of a good gastronome in them.

However, it is important to note that the Ding Chou lack a high rate of ambition and drive compared to those born under the other Ding Pillars. This often makes them a little fragile and as a result, they seldom make heady and flashy achievements in their life or career.

On a separate note, they must be careful not to allow their determination to become overbearing. When their determination oversteps its boundaries, they become excessively stubborn and self-willed. This excessiveness may be their undoing. Only when they maintain a healthy balance of grit and sensibility, with an openness to accept constructive criticism from others, they will be able to thrive in their life or career pursuits.

Key Character Traits of the Ding Chou 丁丑: Overall
• Enthusiastic • Creative • Independent • Gregarious • Optimistic • Inventive • Disciplined

Work Life

丁丑

Ding Chou

Professional Self

Intuitively business-oriented, Ding Chou individuals are endowed with the ability to see opportunities when others cannot. This mind frame makes them dynamic executives and managers who would be great working inside of large corporations. Determination coupled with exceptional leadership skills creates an atmosphere in which they can achieve anything. Once they set their minds to something, they can advance in all areas of life.

Those who work with the Ding Chou appreciate their disciplined and broadminded approach for implementing original ideas. In times of crisis, they are the ones anyone can count on to solve the problem instead of panicking. They see problems as a challenge, not an impediment.

The Ding Chou would be wise not to overlook or underestimate any opportunity, no matter how minor it may seem at the moment. They can cultivate amazing results if they could only recognize the value of situations. When they remain optimistic about their plans there is really nothing stopping the Ding Chou from succeeding.

Due to their inventive minds and progressive outlook, it is not uncommon to find the Ding Chou researching the latest news in information technology. They may also be found blazing the trails for emerging industries.

They should avoid getting into a rut or becoming discouraged about situations. This may cause them to neglect the need for hard work, perseverance, and determination necessary to succeed.

Furthermore, they need to discount their first impulse of readily giving up or taking the easy way out. Instead, they should practice mental detachment. This will give the Ding Chou the confidence needed in order to see situations through and achieve success.

Career Options

Quite a few careers would be suitable for the Ding Chou. They may want to consider using their problem solving skills to excel as specialists, advisors, counselors, or entrepreneurs. Because of their wide range of interests, they could also be satisfied working in sales, promotion, or advertising.

Buried inside of the Ding Chou is a desire for self-expression. This self-expression can be fulfilled through careers in writing, art, music, food, gourmet, acting, dancing, singing or drama. Other similar, yet suitable careers would be design or fashion.

Some born within the Ding Chou Pillar may find themselves inextricably drawn to careers in philosophy, spirituality, or metaphysics. As they mature, their humanitarian side may attract them to vocations in psychology and counseling.

Regardless of which career they choose, they won't achieve satisfying and sustainable success unless they vow to work hard, and complete the job.

Key Character Traits of the Ding Chou 丁丑: Work life

Positive

- Calm
- Disciplined
- Broad-minded
- Inventive
- Intelligent
- Meticulous

Negative

- Snobbish
- Lack of clarity
- Domineering
- Egotistical
- Impatient

Love and Relationships

丁
丑

Ding Chou

Love

Ding Chou individuals are romantic and cherish their intimate relations. Although loving, they can become wrought with inner conflict and overwhelmed with feelings of inhibition. Because of this, it is often difficult for them to express their deep and powerful emotions.

The Ding Chou individuals are generally fun-loving character that craves for adventure or excitement in life. One can't help but feeling or rather, admire the fact that the Ding Chou know more about having fun than they do. Their bold attitude and get-up-and-go way of living attract thrones of admirers, many of which are also fun-seeker as they are. The Ding Chou can be charming, generous and giving to the one they love, and this makes them the more desirable one in the relationship.

Acquaintances

Those born under the Ding Chou Pillar are exceptionally friendly and affectionate. They also accept others without prejudice and are able to make friends with just about everyone.

Ding Chou individuals make loyal and trustworthy friends, who are willing to use their entire arsenal of personal resources to help those they love. Their natural gregarious nature provides them with a host of friends and a myriad of admirers.

They are often considered ahead of their time with unconventional and off-beat ideas. Their love for originality causes them to enjoy the company of other unconventional individuals with whom they can match wits.

They are honest in their communications with others and prefer to be direct and frank in their conversations. This is why their friends clamor for their attention and advice.

There are those who are waiting to take advantage of their kindness, however, they should never let that blind them to the many more friends who sincerely love them.

Family

Individuals of this Pillar are unpretentious, sensitive, and sincerely care about the welfare of their family.
They may find love and marriage later in life, which usually occurs in their favor. Love acquired later in life ensures that the marriage will be lasting and loving.

Men benefit from marrying a Ding Chou female because they bring luck to their husbands. Additionally, wives born under this Pillar excel at managing the household.

There is also the danger that the Ding Chou spouse may leave the marriage during the good moments. Fortune seems to go to their heads as they abandon everything they have built and accumulated up to that point.

Ding Chou parents love their children deeply and take good care of them. In return, their children will be loving and appreciative. They may have many children, however, it is unlikely that more than one offspring will achieve wealth and success.

Key Character Traits of the Ding Chou 丁丑: Love & Relationships

- Kind
- Loving
- Loyal
- Honest
- Charismatic
- Affectionate

Famous Personalities

Thomas Edison - American inventor and businessman. He invented the phonography, the motion picture camera, and the light bulb. He is the most prolific inventor in history.

Prince Andrew - Duke of York. He is the third child of Queen Elizabeth II. He is the fourth in line to the throne.

Source: Wikipedia (June 2013)

Technical Analysis

丁丑

Ding Chou

BaZi Day Pillar Analytics 日柱分析

時 Hour	日 Day	月 Month	年 Year	
	日元 DM **丁** Ding Yin Fire			天干 Heavenly Stems
	墓 Grave **丑** Chou Ox Yin Earth			地支 Earthly Branches
	辛 Xin - Metal 才 IW · 己 Ji - Earth 食 EG · 癸 Gui - Water 殺 7K			藏干 Hidden Stems

丁丑

Fire Ox

In general, the Ding Chou 丁丑 Pillar is considered a weak Fire Pillar. This is because in the BaZi Chart, the Ding 丁 (Fire) sits on the Chou 丑 (Ox) and is not Rooted 通根 in the Branch. However, this Pillar is resting with the Indirect Wealth 偏財星 Seven Killings 七殺星 and Eating God 食神星 Stars in the BaZi Chart. When these stars are awakened, this combination denotes a person has great potential in most integral aspects of life. This means that the Ding Chou can very well achieve a satisfying and fulfilling career, business or family. This is because these Stars produce each other to create a great Chart.

The Ding Chou individual is an idealistic dreamer. They are inventive and imaginative, and they have an inherently gentle nature. They are always very conscious of the feelings of others. All these stemmed from the nature of the hidden Eating God Star.

They are capable of revolutionary and groundbreaking discoveries. They are at their best when experimenting and working with new ideas and concepts. When they are on a personal quest they will be decisive and forceful. They have extraordinary clarity and depth of vision.

The Ding Chou individual is however always caught between their powerful independent qualities and their deep sensitivity. They may be original thinkers but they are also very easily influenced by peer pressure and they often need to work hard to establish their own unique identity. They will appear to the world to be confident, resourceful and resilient, seldom revealing the emotional turmoil and vulnerability underneath.

They are deeply affected by their environment and the company they keep. The right friendships and partnerships in which the other individual is encouraging and supportive will allow the Ding Chou to shine. Whereas involvements where there is a lack of trust of where the other party is disparaging or critical could leave the Ding Chou feeling discouraged or fearful.

It is only through experience that the Ding Chou will learn to reconcile the two sides of their personality. They need to learn to trust their own feelings and intuitions. Until they have succeeded they likely to be moody and restless.

Technical Observations

In this BaZi Chart, the Jia 甲 Wood and Geng 庚 Metal are used to produce the Fire Drilling from Wood 鑽燧於木 and Fire Drilling from Stone 激煙於石 formations respectively. It is vital that the Fire 火 and Earth 土 elements remain dry in the Chart. However, the Ding 丁 Fire will risk being extinguished if this Ding Chou 丁丑 Pillar is found with the Chen 辰 (Dragon), Zi 子 (Rat), or with Water 水 element/luck in the Luck Pillars. This will cause the Fire element of this Chart to become imbalanced and thus, bring upon feelings of instability and confusion to this individual. It is also unfavorable if this Pillar clashes with the Resource 印星 Star as well. Unless it is supported by the presence of the Wood 木 element, this Chart would be indicative of a person with a shorter lifespan or perhaps, poor health.

The Ding Chou person possess the potential to develop stomach-related diseases, if the contamination of the Gui 癸 Water with Ji 己 Earth in the Chou 丑 (Ox) Branch is seen in this BaZi Chart. It is not improbable that they will succumb to illness, especially when the Wood element is not present in the Chart to act as a filter.

The Ding Chou Pillar sits on the Storage 庫 of Metal, and this signifies an abundance of wealth, denoting the possibility for the Ding Chou to amass assets and wealth in life. However, to fulfill the wealth potential, the Si 巳 (Snake) needs to be present in the Chart. But take note, where too much Fire element is found in the Chart, Ding Chou individuals are more likely to fall sick in the process of accumulating wealth. This is especially true if the presence of Wei 未 (Goat) is also found in the Chart. To prevent this Clash, an arbitrator element needs to be

The BaZi 60 Pillars Life Analysis Method

present in the Chart - in this case, a Mao 卯 (Rabbit) or a Hai 亥 (Pig) would turn things around.

Just like the Ding Hai 丁亥, the Ding Chou women will be hard-working mothers with not much personal time allocated for their children. When the Mao 卯 (Rabbit) Branch is seen, the husband's mother will be the one who will take care of the children.

With regards to marriage, the Water element will represent the Ding Chou's husband. The Ding Chou's husband Star is inside the Grave 墓 position in the 12 Growth Phases Theory of BaZi and this denotes a weak affinity with husband. This could also mean that their husband may risk serious injury in the future if the husband Palace is clashed and harmed at the same time with the Luck Pillars.

It is favorable for this Pillar to meet with additional Geng 庚, Jia 甲, Wood 木, Fire 火 and Earth 土 elements in the Luck Pillars, as this would counter the negative influences in the Chart. It will be unfavorable if this Pillar meets with excessive Xin 辛 and Water 水 elements in the Luck Pillars as this will diminish the positive elements for this person.

The Ding Chou born in the Spring and Summer months are more likely to enjoy the good life without too much obstacles in their way. Born in the Winter or Autumn months, these individuals have a higher chance of being wealthy and prosperous. Born during the day (5AM – 5PM), the Ding Chou possesses a good outlook regarding their fortune. Born at night (5PM – 5AM), these individuals can anticipate great fortune in their life. It is less favourable to be born in the Chou 丑(Ox) month, as life may present many, many challenges and obstacles along the way.

Unique 60 Pillar Combinations

This section covers the relationships between the individual pillar under this elemental polarity and several other pillars found in the 60 Jia Zi cycle.

丁
丑

Ding Chou

Heaven Combine Earth Punish 天合地刑
Ding Chou 丁丑 (Fire Ox) + Ren Xu 壬戌 (Water Dog)

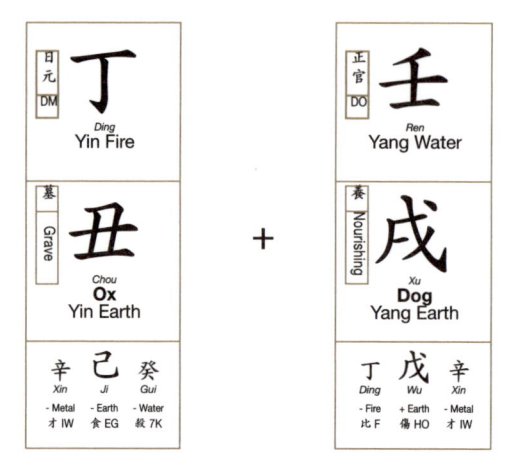

日元 DM	丁 Ding Yin Fire		正官 DO	壬 Ren Yang Water
墓 Grave	丑 Chou Ox Yin Earth	+	養 Nourishing	戌 Xu Dog Yang Earth
辛 Xin - Metal 才 IW	己 Ji - Earth 食 EG	癸 Gui - Water 殺 7K	丁 Ding - Fire 比 F	戊 Wu + Earth 傷 HO	辛 Xin - Metal 才 IW

This Pillar combines with the Heavenly Stem to form a Punishment 刑 with the Earthly Branch. Found in the Ding Chou chart it indicates an external illusion of happiness that disguises unseen emotional stress or pain. The combination of the Heaven Stem with the Earth Branch denotes individuals who hide their problems and put on a cheerful facade for the outside world.

This combination may appear in the BaZi Natal Chart in the Year, Month or Hour Pillars. It may also be found in the Luck Pillars and the Annual Pillar.

Found in Year Pillar of the Natal Chart, it is an indication the Ding Chou has a positive rapport with their grandparents, at least superficially. The reality will be far more complicated and there will be negative emotions hidden below the surface.

When this configuration is seen in the Month Pillar, the Ding Chou will appear to all the world to have a good relationship with their parents. But again, there will be unseen tensions that would likely stem from unresolved issues.

When this configuration is present in the Month Pillar the underlying tension could instead be revealed in the career of the Ding Chou. This may appear in the form of office politics. The casual observer would doubtless not detect a problem but the office relationships would be superficial and strained. The problems are likely to stem from the Ding Chou themselves.

When this configuration appears in the Hour Pillar, the Ding Chou may be in the habit of promising too much and delivering too little. The individual may be agreeing to undertakings in order to keep the peace but they will run the risk of creating discord and distrust if they do not learn to take on only those tasks they know they can complete.

When discovered in the Luck Pillar, this configuration is indicative of a situation in which everything is running according to plan but the Ding Chou cannot believe they deserve this good fortune. Their colleagues and friends may look to them with admiration but the Ding Chou will not share their confidence. They may unconsciously sabotage their own success with this attitude.

When Heaven Combine Earth Punish is found in the Annual Pillar, it signals a year in which plans and hopes must be postponed or go off course at the eleventh hour. It is possible that the Ding Chou, sensing again that perhaps their good luck may not hold, may be prone to act too carefully and that this fear and over-caution is in itself the cause of the problems. There may also be stress and tension in the workplace and the Ding Chou is advised to try to keep their emotions and reactions under control.

Heaven Combine Earth Harm 天合地害
Ding Chou 丁丑 (Fire Ox) + Ren Wu 壬午 (Water Horse)

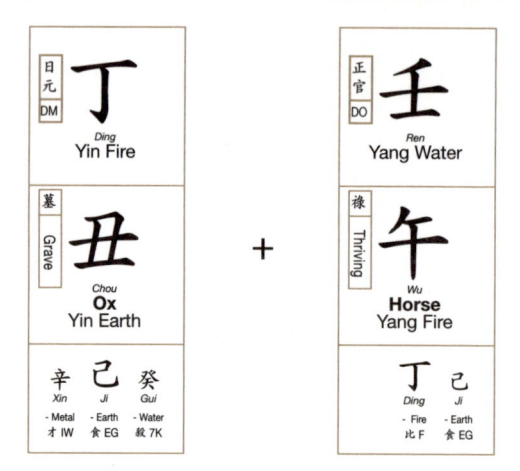

日元 DM	丁	Ding	Yin Fire
墓 Grave	丑	Chou **Ox**	Yin Earth

辛 Xin	己 Ji	癸 Gui
- Metal 才 IW	- Earth 食 EG	- Water 殺 7K

\+

正官 DO	壬	Ren	Yang Water
祿 Thriving	午	Wu **Horse**	Yang Fire

丁 Ding	己 Ji
- Fire 比 F	- Earth 食 EG

This Pillar combines with the Heavenly Stem to form a Harm 害 with the Ding Chou's Earthly Branch. The presence of this configuration is an indication that the Ding Chou may appear to be happy and have a positive outlook due to the presence of the Heavenly Stem but they will be hiding feeling of uncertainty and distrust.

This combination can be found in the BaZi Natal Chart in the Year, Month and Year Pillars as well as the Luck and Annual Pillars.

It indicates the individual may appear to have a very close relationship with their grandparents when it is found in the Year Pillar. In private however the relationship with be far from satisfactory and both parties may be uncertain about the bond they share.

If found in the Month Pillar, this configuration can be an indication that what may appear to be an outwardly positive relationship with parents or superiors at work, may act to disguise a measure of distrust and confusion.

Found in the Hour Pillar and the outside world will believe the Ding Chou to have a good relationship with their children behind closed doors. Both sides will sense that there is something out of place. Additionally a similar situation could arise at the Ding Chou's workplace in connection to their employees, suppliers or clients.

When seen in the Luck Pillar this configuration high hopes and great success leaving the Ding Chou with a feeling that far from being victorious they have instead become the victims of the situation. They will feel jaded and fail to find peace of mind in their achievements.

The year will start out with great promise, when this configuration is in the Annual Pillar, but it is likely to end on a note of disappointment. It is likely that the year has delivered exactly as expected but the Ding Chou has allowed themselves to become envious of others and this has distorted their judgment of their accomplishments.

Heaven Friend Earth Clash 天比地沖
Ding Chou 丁丑 (Fire Ox) + Ding Wei 丁未 (Fire Goat)

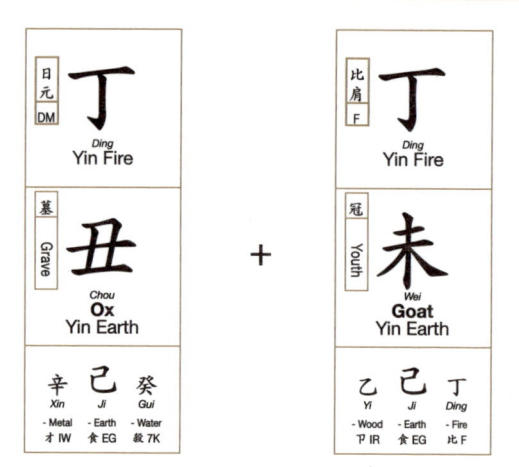

This configuration is an indication that what may begin well with positive agreements may eventually end in a disagreement. It also suggests that though the Ding Chou is very active they may fail to produce anything tangible from their efforts. They may also discover that what has actually been promised does not materialize in the manner they expected.

This situation carried with it a great sense of the unexpected. Since the unexpected can be positive as well as negative the ultimate outcome will depend on whether the Heavenly Stem is favorable. A favorable Heavenly Stem will indicate a positive conclusion.

Should this configuration be found in the Ding Chou's BaZi Natal Chart in the Year Pillar, their relationships with their grandparents may be very positive in the outset but could take an unexpected turn for the worse.

The same holds true for their relationship with their parents if this configuration is located in the Month Pillar. An event or a mishap may have an unexpected impact on these connections. The same effect may be apparent in the Ding Chou's workplace.

Should this configuration appear in the Hour Pillar, the individual's ideas and contributions to the world will be affected by some anticipated turn of events. Equally there may be surprises in store with regard to their relationship with their children.

If this configuration appears in the Luck Pillar of the Ding Chou, the individual will go through a period of growth, progress and positive change. The process will be slow and even painful but the ultimate outcome will be a positive.

If in the Annual Pillar, this configuration suggests that the Ding Chou will face many unexpected twists and turns throughout the year. They fight some private battles but they will learn a great deal from the experience. They are advised to have a little faith in themselves and to be patient as things will eventually blow over.

Heaven and Earth Clash 天沖地冲
Ding Chou 丁丑 (Fire Ox) + Gui Wei 癸未 (Water Goat)

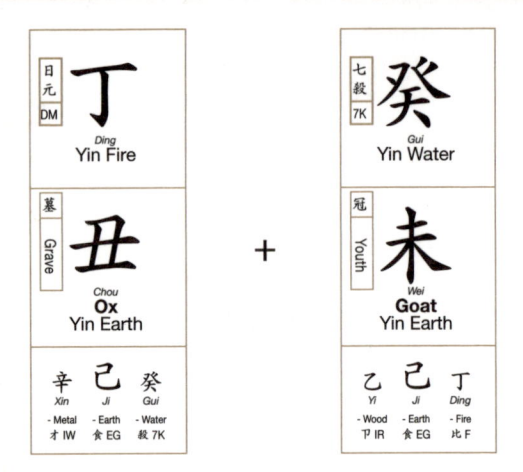

Ding 丁 (DM) Yin Fire	Gui 癸 (7K) Yin Water
Chou 丑 (Grave) Ox Yin Earth	Wei 未 (Youth) Goat Yin Earth
辛 Xin - Metal 才 IW / 己 Ji - Earth 食 EG / 癸 Gui - Water 殺 7K	乙 Yi - Wood 卩 IR / 己 Ji - Earth 食 EG / 丁 Ding - Fire 比 F

The Heaven and Earth Clash Pillar is a formation where the Day Pillar clashes with the Gui Wei 癸未 Pillar. This is known as the Fan Yin 反吟 and is considered to be an undesirable formation as it will diminish any of the good qualities of an individual's Day Pillar. This has a negative impact on the individual's chances of achieving success on their own merits. It is recommended of the Ding Chou to check the Charts of those connected with them for this formation as another individual with this Pillar in their Chart may be a negative influence and could be the source of poor advice. This can also be known as the Mutual Exchange Goat Blade 互換羊刃 formation in different circumstances, depending on the overall view of the Chart.

In whichever position in the Natal Chart, this configuration indicates a lack of affinity with the person or persons represented by the specific Pillar in which it appears. If this combination is seen in the Year Pillar, it suggests a less-than-desirable relationship with the grandparents, either because there is friction between them or that they have never met. As the Year Pillar also governs one's social circle, it denotes that the individual may not have any close friendships in life.

In the Month Pillar, it denotes a strained connection with parents. It also refers to the poor affinity with superiors or peers as the Month Pillar also represents a person's work and career. This configuration could mean that the individual does not receive much respect or support from the people at work.

When in the Hour Pillar, it can be an indication of a lack of affinity with children or work subordinates. As the Hour Pillar also governs one's hopes and dreams, this configuration here would mean that the individual may have lost direction or sense of purpose in life, and is clueless as his/her next step.

In the Luck Pillar, where this combination is present, it symbolizes a point in time where painful changes, stress and obstacles are apparent.

In the Annual Pillars, if this combination is seen, the individual is advised to keep to their status quo and deter from committing to any drastic life-altering decision for the year. Major decision in important life aspects should be delayed.

Heaven Counter Earth Clash 天剋地沖
Ding Chou 丁丑 (Fire Ox) + Xin Wei 辛未 (Metal Goat)

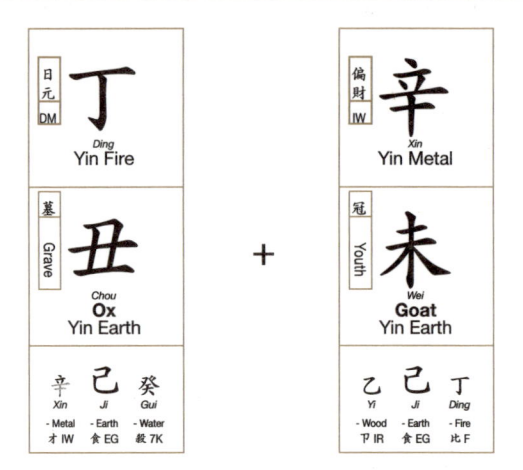

The Heaven Counter Earth Clash Pillar is a configuration where the Day Pillar is going against the Xin Wei 辛未. This is not to be mistaken for the Heaven and Earth Clash formation. In this formation, it is the Ding Chou individual who is in control.

When this Pillar appears it symbolizes either controlling or competitive nature. The individual is likely to pursue victory with passion and drive. These individual's may be prone to being rash or impatient but they also possess great entrepreneurial acumen. This configuration is often thought to be an indication of wealth and achievement. In certain circumstances, this is also known as the Mutual Exchange Goat Blade configuration, depending on the overall of the BaZi Chart.

The Heaven and Earth Clash Pillar can be found in the BaZi Natal Chart in the Year, Month and Hour Pillars and it can appear in both the Luck and Annual Pillars.

When it is located in the Year Pillar, it denotes the Ding Chou have influential friends. These friends will be willing to pass on their wisdom and experience; their advice may prove to be invaluable.

It is thought that individuals with this configuration in the Month Pillar of their Chart are likely to have good business instincts. They will enjoy working with money and will have a gift for making a profit. That said, they should also remember not to allow greed to overcome them.

Should this Pillar be placed in the Hour Pillar, the individual will be more than passionate about their work it will be their singular interest and pursuit in life. They will be married to their work and have little time for other relationships. Their bonds with their families and friends are likely to suffer.

When placed in the Luck Pillar, the Heaven Counter Earth Clash foretells a ten-year period of excellent financial returns. The Ding Chou can expect to see many opportunities for advancement and investment.

Wealth-related opportunities are also promised when this configuration is in the Annual Pillar. This may be the beginning of new business ventures as well as the creation of new partnerships. The year will be marked by achievement but this period of intense activity may however be rather stressful and the individual may neglect their personal relationships.

Heaven and Earth Unity 天同地比
Ding Chou 丁丑 (Fire Ox) + Ding Chou 丁丑 (Wood Ox)

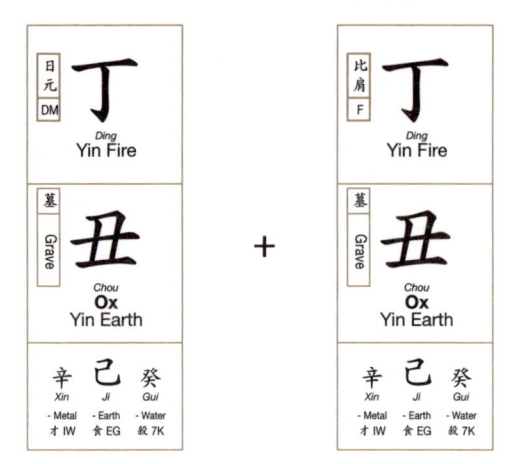

This combination is known by two different references. It is traditionally called the Fu Yin 伏吟 when it appears in the BaZi Chart. It is also known as the Hidden Warning Pillar. The appearance of the Heaven and Earth Unity has two potential interpretations. Either a great sadness will shroud the Ding Chou or they will meet with a series of emotional events or trying circumstances.

When found in the Year Pillar the Ding Chou may suffer the loss of the previously good bond with their grandparents. Alternatively the relationship may never have had the chance to develop as it is possible that the individual may never have met their grandparents.

When found in the Month Pillar, the Ding Chou may struggle to establish a positive relationship with their parents. These problems may be connected to the family business or matters of inheritance.

94 The BaZi 60 Pillars Life Analysis Method

If the Heaven and Earth Unity is found in the Hour Pillar, it may be that the individual is not as close to their children as they would like. Their children may no longer live at home or they may have been raised by their grandparents. Alternatively the individual may not be biologically capable of having children.

When this configuration is found in the Luck Pillar, it indicates the important of the spiritual to the individual. They may become devoutly religious or develop an independent or unconventional sense of their spirituality that is equally important to them. Alternatively they may become very focused on their health, diet and fitness. It is sadly not unusual for those with this configuration in the Luck Pillar to lose a parent.

Appearing in the Annual Pillar, the Heaven and Earth Unity denotes a year of achievement and career success. The individual will see a growth in their material wealth but emotionally straining events will cast a shadow over the year.

Heaven and Earth Combo 天地相合
Ding Chou 丁丑 (Fire Ox) + Ren Zi 壬子 (Water Rat)

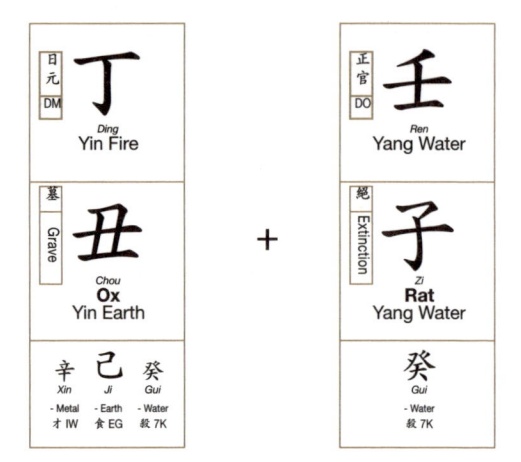

日元 DM	丁 Ding Yin Fire		正官 DO	壬 Ren Yang Water
墓 Grave	丑 Chou **Ox** Yin Earth	**+**	絕 Extinction	子 Zi **Rat** Yang Water
辛 Xin - Metal 才 IW	己 Ji - Earth 食 EG	癸 Gui - Water 殺 7K		癸 Gui - Water 殺 7K

This combination is possibly the most fortuitous. It symbolizes strong bonds throughout all relationships in all areas of the Ding Chou's life. These positive relationships will impact upon the Ding Chou personal and professional lives bringing them success and happiness.

When seen in the chart of someone connected to the Ding Chou it is an indication that these two will share a particular affinity and that this individual will be able to offer help and support when needed.

Should the arrangement be found in the Year Pillar the individual will have supportive ties with their grandparents or their friends. They can also look forward to enjoying a well-place social status.

When this appears in the Month Pillar it foretells that the individual will have an excellent affinity with their parents as well as with those in authority in their workplace.

The location of the Heaven and Earth Combine in the Hour Pillar predicts good relations with their children and a rapport with their staff or employees.

The appearance of this configuration in the Luck or Annual Pillars, the individual will experience luck and happiness in their romances and personal relationships. They are also likely to enjoy professional success through partnerships or joint ventures.

丁丑

Fire
Ox

Mutual Exchange Goat Blade 互換羊刃
Ding Chou 丁丑 (Fire Ox) + Gui Wei 癸未 (Water Goat)

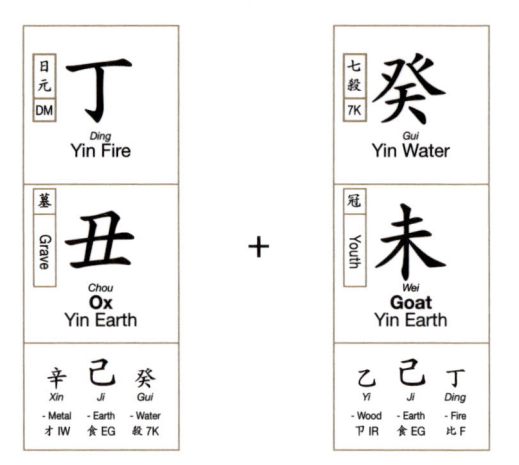

日元 DM	丁 Ding Yin Fire		七殺 7K	癸 Gui Yin Water
墓 Grave	丑 Chou Ox Yin Earth	+	冠 Youth	未 Wei Goat Yin Earth
辛 Xin - Metal 才 IW	己 Ji - Earth 食 EG	癸 Gui - Water 殺 7K	乙 Yi - Wood 卩 IR	己 Ji - Earth 食 EG	丁 Ding - Fire 比 F

This configuration has a similar impact to the Rob Wealth Goat Blade 劫財羊刃. The effect of this one is more subtle.

This combination may indicate loss of health or vitality, possibly through accident. This may be in connection with the individuals represented by the Pillars in which the configuration appears.

These people will not be intentionally trying to harm or injure the Ding Chou. It simply means when the Ding Chou faces a greater chance of being involved in accidents which may have an impact on their health when those people are around them.

Rob Wealth Goat Blade 劫財羊刃
Ding Chou 丁丑 (Fire Ox) + Bing Wu 丙午 (Fire Horse)

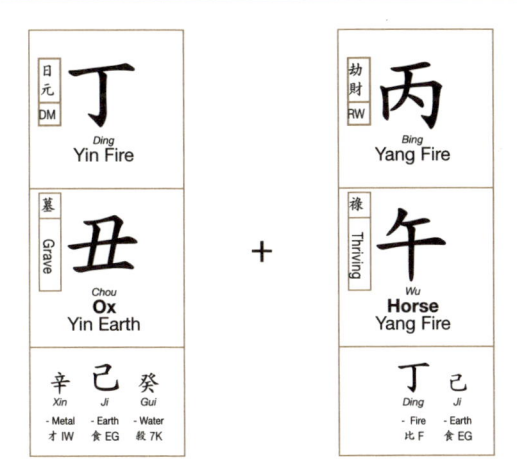

日元 DM	丁 Ding Yin Fire		劫財 RW	丙 Bing Yang Fire
墓 Grave	丑 Chou Ox Yin Earth	+	祿 Thriving	午 Wu Horse Yang Fire
辛 Xin - Metal 才 IW	己 Ji - Earth 食 EG	癸 Gui - Water 殺 7K	丁 Ding - Fire 比 F	己 Ji - Earth 食 EG

If you're a Ding Chou, you do not want to see a Bing Wu 丙午 Pillar in your Chart. The Rob Wealth Goat Blade 劫財羊刃 Pillar has the impact of causing the Ding Chou to lose money and experience financial losses. When found in another person's Chart, it is likely that this individual will be the cause of these monetary damage. This may not be intentional on their part and the Ding Chou themselves may not be aware of it at the time. The individual could be a source of poor career advice, or it may be that the Ding Chou tends to spend more money while with them.

丁卯

Ding Mao

丁丑 Ding Chou　丁卯 Ding Mao　丁巳 Ding Si　丁未 Ding Wei　丁酉 Ding You　丁亥 Ding Hai

Getting to Know
Ding Mao 丁卯 (Fire Rabbit)

丁卯

Ding Mao

Positive Imagery

八字一柱論命法

丁卯
Fire
Rabbit

Negative Imagery

八字一柱論命法

丁卯

Fire Rabbit

Getting to Know
Ding Mao 丁卯 (Fire Rabbit)

General Observations:

Much like its imagery of the glowing embers from a scented incense stick, the Ding Mao is traditionally considered the most beautiful of all Ding 丁 characters.

Ding Mao individuals are outspoken and independent. They have natural linguistic skills and a great gift for written and verbal communication, while their exceptional mental abilities enable them to express their ideas in a clear and concise manner. As they are incredibly inventive and original, their minds are often full of progressive ideas and they are frequently considered to be ahead of their time. The Ding Mao individual has an innate ability to acquire knowledge from a wide variety of sources and they are happiest when doing so. Often Ding Mao individuals will have a photographic memory and a natural ability to absorb and process information which has earned them a reputation for being quite the intellectual.

Creative and adaptable, the Ding Mao has a powerhouse of intellectual abilities that will often lead them to becoming pioneers in their field. They can be incredibly enthusiastic about new projects and their keen and alert, highly analytical minds have tremendous potential in a variety of careers. They have a great gift for recognizing new opportunities and are often able to spot business and economic trends at the earliest stages, with the capacity to think and act fast they have what it takes to turn these opportunities into profitability and career success.

The Ding Mao may be perceived as a people person. They have the ability to network and build new connections and open new doors. Likened to a matchstick that is able to start new fires without diminishing its own, the Ding Mao individual is often able to inspire those around them and use this team working to push projects and ventures forward.

The Ding Mao person's incredible mental gifts will often mean that they are easily bored with repetitive or mundane tasks and they will need constant stimulation in order to be fully engaged. It will be vital for them to be inspired if they are to be able to apply themselves and this may lead them to taking on a number of different projects as their interest is forever being sparked by new ideas. Once they are focused however there is almost no limit to what they can achieve.

For all their positive qualities the Ding Mao individual's own perfectionism may lead them to doubt their own abilities and pull the reins on their progress. Incredibly idealistic, with very high expectations of themselves and others, the Ding Mao individual may be wrought with doubts and inner conflicts. They may lack in confidence and struggle to perceive their tremendous strength and talent and these insecurities may also impact upon their relationships with others making them suspicious and, at times, even withdrawn. The Ding Mao has a great need for the love and support of others in order to feel secure and to have the courage to discover their true potential. They need to steer clear of negative thoughts and to stay positive. They will often benefit from having a teacher or mentor to nurture and guide them into finding their true path.

Spiritual enlightenment may well also assist the Ding Mao individual to find harmony in their lives and to gain a control of their vulnerabilities. If they are able to achieve a sense of inner peace and develop faith in themselves and their instincts, they will easily be able to turn their idealistic dreams into concrete reality.

The Ding Mao individual will often become very wealthy and they have a great appreciation of the finer things in life. They are particularly intrigued by food and in taste and texture. They will often take an interest in new and exciting cuisine and will always be interested to try foods from different places around the world. They will be motivated to search for new and exquisite taste experiences and they are likely to know the locations of all the best restaurants as well as being a dab hand in the kitchen. Women of this Pillar are often excellent household managers and their love of food and cooking may mean that they enjoy some of the domestic duties that others would consider a chore.

The Ding Mao individual will benefit from taking some time to consider their wellbeing and future security. They may have a tendency toward ill health and it would be advisable for them to take pains to ensure they eat well and get adequate exercise. They will also benefit from financial planning in order to enjoy a prosperous old age.

Creative and sociable with incredible intellectual abilities the Ding Mao has the ability to achieve almost anything that they put their minds to. With the support and encouragement of their loved ones and confidence in their own talents, they are likely to find that their potential is almost boundless.

Key Character Traits of the Ding Mao 丁卯: Overall

- Thoughtful
- Compassionate
- Opinionated
- Analytical
- Good Memory
- Independent
- Creative
- Liberal
- Spiritual

八字一柱論命法

丁卯
Fire Rabbit

Work Life

丁卯

Ding Mao

Professional Self

Ding Mao individuals have the inner drive necessary to create successful careers for themselves. Although capable of success in a variety of vocations, their disdain for taking orders makes them more ideal for either entrepreneurship or any career that provides much freedom.

These individuals are among the first to recognize an opportunity. With their practical outlook, organizational skills and executive abilities, they can turn any opportunity into success. Ding Mao individuals are noted for thinking on a grand scale and being able to carry the concept to completion.

Possibly, it would be wise for them to consider participating in fund management or banking. Their ability to understand and crunch numbers, recognize business and economic trends gives them an edge in this field over others.

Due to their empathy and diplomacy skills, they may want to examine the option of working closely with other people. Fields that draw on their strength in communication and teamwork would make the most suitable platform to begin a great career ahead.

Career Options

The Ding Mao thrive in various career fields. Due to their multi-talented creative abilities, the Ding Mao may do extremely well in music, art, writing, acting and directing.

Since their communication skills are excellent, they may want to consider entering into sales, advertising or media industry. They can also use their highly developed communication and problem-solving skills for careers in business, banking, mutual funds, philosophy or education as a teacher, lecturer or a successful entrepreneur.

They have innate knowledge and ability to undergird any project. These traits would make them excellent managers and entrepreneurs, all of which consistent with their craving for success and achievements. They will also find a great career as brokers, fund managers and bankers. This is because their strong analytical thinking helps them to easily grasp the market and economic trends better than others.

Ding Mao individuals with more of a technical-related interest may benefit greatly from a career in computers, finance or engineering. If they want the best of both worlds, they could combine their technical and creative talents by pursuing a career in computer games.

八字一柱論命法

丁卯
Fire Rabbit

Key Character Traits of the Ding Mao 丁卯: Work life

Positive

- Ambitious
- Skilled communicators
- Good problem-solvers
- Practical
- Diplomatic

Negative

- Rebellious
- Poor planners
- Controlling
- Stubborn

Love and Relationships

丁卯

Ding Mao

Love

When Ding Mao individuals fall in love, they are dutiful, devoted and sacrificial on behalf of their partner. Their partner treasures them for these traits, but somehow the Ding Mao can be very stubborn at times and unwilling to change their fixed ideals. This often frustrates their partner, causing them to appear uncommitted.

Moreover, Ding Mao individuals live a very busy life and seldom have time for romance. Business and career take over important precedence in their lives. They may view romantic time as "unproductive" and would rather be doing something else besides just sitting in front of the fire place.

Acquaintances

Ding Mao individuals have a sociable, friendly and charismatic personality. They are great at entertaining others and will use this to channel their positive expression.

They make it a point to surround themselves with individuals who are ambitious, hardworking and success oriented. Because of this, prestige and money could be important factors in any of their relationships.

Many describe those within this Pillar "lucky" when it comes to relating with people. This luck is actually their confidence and friendliness coming to the fore.

If a Ding Mao becomes restless, they should perhaps look around them. This may surface due to their desire to satisfy their adventurous spirit.

Family

Their family relies on them for generosity, love and support. They are devoted to their family and can wield influence, admiration and respect within the family circle. For their children, they are best role model there is, and this admiration translates into a desire for the children to fill the big shoes.

Although devoted to their marriages, their unions are typically ordinary and average. Often more devoted to their career or business, the Ding Mao can be perceived as non-committal although it is in their nature to give more for their professional stride. It recommended for the Ding Mao to make time for their family, as professional success alone doesn't warrant lasting happiness in life.

Key Character Traits of the Ding Mao 丁卯: Love & Relationships
• Devoted • Caring • Love of family • Supportive • Charismatic

八字一柱論命法

丁卯
Fire Rabbit

Famous Personalities

Tunku Abdul Rahman Putra Al-Haj – The 1st Prime Minister of Malaysia, also known as the Father of Independence. He was also a lawyer before he went into politics.

Tina Turner - a singer, dancer, actress, author, and choreographer. Her career has spanned more than half a century, earning her widespread recognition and numerous awards.

Source: Wikipedia (June 2013)

丁卯
Fire Rabbit

Technical Analysis

丁卯

Ding Mao

BaZi Day Pillar Analytics 日柱分析

時 Hour	日 Day	月 Month	年 Year	
	丁 **Ding** Yin Fire (日元 DM)			天干 Heavenly Stems
	卯 **Mao** Rabbit Yin Wood (病 Sick)			地支 Earthly Branches
	乙 Yi - Wood 乙 IR			藏干 Hidden Stems

丁卯 Fire Rabbit

八字一柱論命法

The Ding Mao 丁卯 Pillar sits on the Resource Star 印星 and is thought to be supported by the Day Branch. The Resource Star is perceived as being the most important element for the Ding Fire. This is because Ding Fire needs Wood (its Resource element) to survive. By receiving the help of the Resource Star, Ding Mao individuals are likely to be wise, knowledgeable and intelligent. They may even have the opportunity to become the Noblemen to other people if their Pillar meets with the Hai Mao 亥卯 (Pig-Rabbit) Combination or the Yin Mao Chen 寅卯辰 (Tiger-Rabbit-Dragon) Directional Combination in the BaZi Chart. If this Pillar meets with the Indirect Wealth Star 偏財星, they will have the potential to forge an outstanding career.

The Ding Mao aspires to achieve great things. They have high expectations of themselves and those around them. They hold steadfast values and often have great moral and spiritual aspirations. They are innovative,

The BaZi 60 Pillars Life Analysis Method

inventive and progressive. They enjoy learning and are likely to be very knowledgeable with a love of new ideas. When inspired they are enthusiastic and inspirational though they may be inclined to becoming bored or restless if their interest isn't piqued.

Din Mao individuals have a great need for security. This is because of the nature of the Wood element as represented by the Indirect Resource Star. They will work hard for a firm foundation and will make long term plans and financial investments to provide for their futures. Emotional security will be as valuable to them as material security and they will also value a stable and harmonious marriage.

Fortunately the Ding Mao has many of the qualities that one would expect to see in a successful individual. They have natural business acumen, sharp minds and brilliant organizational skills. They also have a gift with words and are exceptional communicators both in written and verbal media.

People of this Pillar may however have a tendency to be rather insecure. This is especially true if there is a presence of You 酉 (Rooster) in the Chart. They may doubt their own abilities and struggle to recognize their great potential. They may also be suspicious of those around them and they will be concerned about the honesty and good intentions of their friends or family. They need to avoid submerging themselves in negative thoughts as this will make them cold, distant and unfulfilled.

Technical Observations

It is favorable if this Ding Mao Chart has the Ren 壬 Water, the Direct Officer Star 正官星 present, as this signifies a successful and celebrated individual. Should the Gui 癸 appear instead of the Ren in this BaZi Chart, it represents a person who is successful through unconventional means. If both Ren and Gui Stems are absent from the Chart, the Fire 火 element will not be controlled and this is likely to cause an imbalance to the Fire element. The effect of this may be for the individual to find that they endure a great deal of difficulty in finding success and fulfillment in life.

The Ding Mao Pillar also sits on the Nobleman Star 貴人星. This denotes that the Ding Mao are endowed with longevity as well as the potential to achieve great success.

The Nobleman [Mao 卯 (Rabbit)] is also the Indirect Resource Star 偏印星, it enhances the intuitive ability of the Ding Mao individuals. However, this formation depends greatly on the quality of the Water 水 element in the BaZi Chart to determine whether this particular trait is actually an advantage or a burden.

The Mao 卯 (Rabbit) also attracts the Hai 亥 (Pig) in a Ding Mao Chart. The Hai 亥 (Pig) carries the Officer Star, which indicates that the individual is likely to be trustworthy and credible. Where this Star is seen in the Chart, the individual will often be able to use it to attract positive relationships that will be of benefit to them as they pursue their careers. If this Star is absent, the Ding Mao may risk meeting with a potentially persistent health issue.

It is desirable for the Ding Mao to meet with additional Metal 金 and Water 水 elements in the Luck Pillars. This condition denotes a period of time where the Ding Mao enjoys good fortune in the form of career success, vibrant health and loving relationships. Should they meet with excessive Wood 木, Fire 火 and Earth 土 elements in the Chart, however, there are less positive implications and it's possible that the individual will face quite a turbulent life.

The Mother star (Resource) sits in the Spouse Palace for the male Ding Mao and this indicates that they are likely to have a very strong relationship with their mother. Due to this, many Ding Mao men are inclined to marry older women who remind them of their mothers, or that they may take a maternal role in the relationship.

Ding Mao individuals who were born in the Spring and Summer months will fare best if they work at continuous improvement and development throughout their lives, and those born in the Autumn and Winter are equally recommended to do the same. Those Ding Mao born during the day time (5AM – 5PM) can should enjoy a reasonable amount of luck in their endeavors, while those born at night (5PM – 5AM) are likely to be persistent and ambitious and they will push for success in their chosen careers. It is not a good sign for a Ding Mao individual to be born in the Chou 丑 (Ox) month as they are likely to find that they struggle to accomplish as much as they desire.

Unique 60 Pillar Combinations

This section covers the relationships between the individual pillar under this elemental polarity and several other pillars found in the 60 Jia Zi cycle.

丁卯

Ding Mao

Heaven Combine Earth Punish 天合地刑
Ding Mao 丁卯 (Fire Rabbit) + Ren Zi 壬子 (Water Rat)

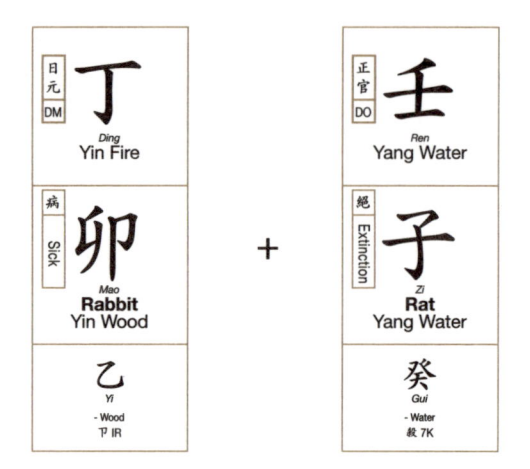

This Pillar combines at the Heavenly Stem, but it forms a Punishment 刑 when it meets with the Earthly Branch. The Heavenly Stem is generally a positive sign but the Punishment suggests negative emotion. This arrangement suggests that the Ding Mao individual will put on a show of happiness while inwardly they will be struggling with feelings of stress and pain.

This configuration may be present in the BaZi Natal Chart in the Year, Month and Hour Pillars as well as their Luck and Annual Pillars.

When it is found in the Year Pillar, it is an indication that beneath the mask of a warm connection, the individual has quite a troubled relationship with their grandparents. This is probably due to issues left unresolved for some time.

The same feeling will apply to their parents if this configuration is in the Month Pillar. On the surface the relationship may appear to be sincere and friendly but there will be tension just beneath that may stem from many misunderstandings.

This placement in the Month Pillar may also have some significance for the individual's career. They are likely to feel quite stressed and unhappy at work. Their work ties may be superficially positive but the individual is likely to lack confidence in their colleagues and they may be involved in some unpleasant office politics. It is likely, in this case however, that it is the Ding Mao's own tendency to be suspicious that is causing the problem. They need to work on their on their own emotional state before they will be able to relax.

This configuration found in the Hour Pillar may be an indication that the Ding Mao try too hard to please. They may take on more than they are able to handle and fail to make good on their promises. They need to learn that their failure to deliver will ultimately create far more bad feeling than simply declining a task they know they cannot complete.

When apparent in the Luck Pillar, this configuration indicates that the individual will accomplish a great deal. They will have the respect and admiration of their peers for their great achievements but they will not themselves have faith their skills and abilities and they will feel unworthy of their good fortune. If they do not develop self-belief they may run the risk of beginning to sabotage their own success.

The Heaven Combine Earth Punish formation, when located in the Annual Pillar, is indicative of cherished plans being put on hold or even being completely derailed. The Ding Mao individual may however be the cause of their own difficulties as their over-cautious nature leads them to making unnecessary changes. They are recommended to remain calm and focused.

Heaven Combine Earth Harm 天合地害
Ding Mao 丁卯 (Fire Rabbit) + Ren Chen 壬辰 (Water Dragon)

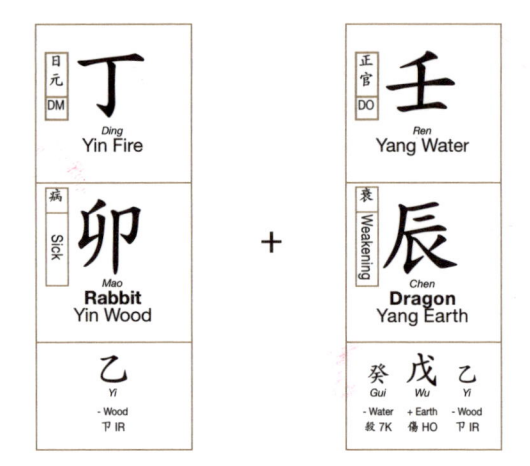

日元 DM	丁 Ding Yin Fire		正官 DO	壬 Ren Yang Water
病 Sick	卯 Mao Rabbit Yin Wood	+	衰 Weakening	辰 Chen Dragon Yang Earth
	乙 Yi – Wood 卯 IR		癸 Gui – Water 殺 7K	戊 Wu + Earth 傷 HO	乙 Yi – Wood 卯 IR

This configuration combines with the Heavenly Stem but forms a Harm 害 with the Ding Mao's Earthly Branch. Again the Heavenly Stem may appear to be a positive but the Harm will carry a damaging effect. The individual is like to put up a strong and optimistic front but deep inside they will be confused and unhappy about their relationships.

This configuration can appear in the BaZi Natal Chart, specifically in the Year, Month or Hour Pillars. It can also be found in the Luck and Annual Pillars.

Placed in the Year Pillar of the Natal Chart, there will be distrust and unhappiness in the individual's relationship with their grandparents. Located in the Month Pillar, there will issues of trust and loyalty affecting their relationship with their parents or their authority figures at work.

In the Hour Pillar, this configuration will suggest that questions over loyalty and trust will plague the individual's relationship with their children. Alternatively, the impact could be felt in their relationship with their employees, clients or suppliers.

Appearing in the Luck Pillar, this configuration indicates what may appear to be a very positive turn of events that somehow leaves the individual feeling abused or victimized. The individual may need to keep his/her chin up and move forward instead of dwelling on the negative.

A good year may end in disappointment if this configuration is found in the Annual Pillar. In this case the individual is advised to focus on the positive and not to allow feelings of jealousy or envy to cloud their perception.

Heaven Friend Earth Clash 天比地沖
Ding Mao 丁卯 (Fire Rabbit) + Ding You 丁酉 (Fire Rooster)

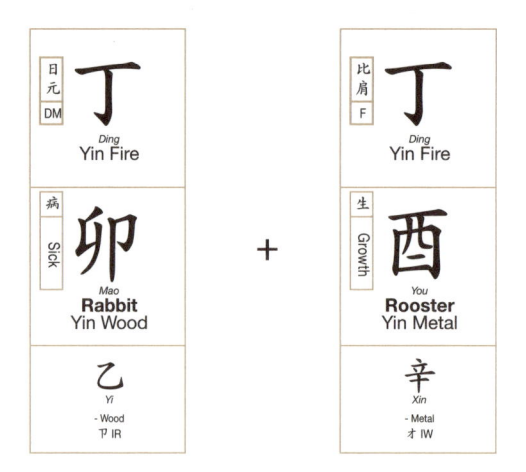

日元 DM	丁 Ding Yin Fire		比肩 F	丁 Ding Yin Fire
病 Sick	卯 Mao **Rabbit** Yin Wood	+	生 Growth	酉 You **Rooster** Yin Metal
	乙 Yi - Wood 卩 IR			辛 Xin - Metal 才 IW

The Heaven Friend Earth Clash formation has the effect of transforming an initial agreement into a disagreement. An unanticipated turn of events may throw plans off course or a promise may fail to live up to expectation causing feelings of disappointment. Though this may be only natural, it is worth noting that surprises aren't always bad and the final outcome will ultimately depend on whether the Heavenly Stem is favorable or unfavorable. If it is favorable, what appears to be a negative outcome may have positive ramifications. Individuals with this configuration in their Chart often find that they work very hard and are frequently very busy but that their efforts fail to produce any tangible results.

This configuration can be found in the BaZi Natal Chart in the Year, Month or Hour Pillars. It can also appear in the Luck Pillars and the Annual Pillar.

Where this configuration appears in the Natal Chart it is an indication that the individual may feel that their plans frequently seem to go astray. They find that this makes them discontented or dissatisfied and these feelings may eventually have an impact on their relationships. In the Year Pillar, they may feel the effects in their relationship with their grandparents. As the Year Pillar also represents social circle and network, the Ding Mao might face certain problems or conflict with their friends.

In the Month Pillar, this combination will instead indicate that the individual is likely to be unhappy about their relationship with their parents. The Month Pillar also represents career and a position here could suggest that the individual will have unsatisfactory relationships with their employers, superiors or colleagues.

When this combination is in the Hour Pillar, it represents a sense of distress and worry with regard to the individual's relationship with their children. The Hour Pillar also signifies hopes and dreams, and a placement here could mean that the individual will feel that something is missing from their lives and they may find that they are forever searching for something more.

Should the Heaven Friend Earth Clash surface in the Luck Pillar, it denotes slow and steady change. This may be difficult time but it will result in positive growth and progression. They are advised to have patience and faith in themselves and be persistent as they will reach their goal eventually.

This configuration located in the Annual Pillar is an indicator that the year will be full of surprises. The individual will have to fight some private battles, but they will emerge enriched by the experience. As the saying goes, "What doesn't kill you, makes you stronger".

Heaven and Earth Clash 天冲地冲
Ding Mao 丁卯 (Fire Rabbit) + Gui You 癸酉 (Water Rooster)

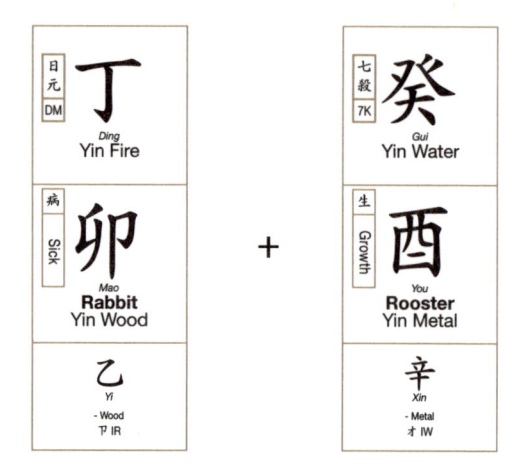

丁 — DM / Ding / Yin Fire
卯 — Sick / Mao / Rabbit / Yin Wood
  乙 Yi - Wood 卩 IR

+

癸 — 7K / Gui / Yin Water
酉 — Growth / You / Rooster / Yin Metal
  辛 Xin - Metal 才 IW

As the Heaven and Earth Clash Pillar is referred to as the Fan Yin 反吟 formation, the presence of it in the Chart erodes many of the good qualities of an individual's Day Pillar. This heavily impairs the individual's chances of achieving success on their own merits.

This arrangement may have a negative effect on the Ding Mao even when it is found in the Charts of those connected to them. These individual may mean no harm but they could be the source of poor advice that may impact on the Ding Mao's career.

This combination may be found in the BaZi Natal Chart in the Year, Month, or Hour Pillars as well as the Luck or Annual Pillars.

If it is found in the Year Pillar, this configuration is an indication that the individual's relationship with their grandparents may become a problem for them. As this Pillar also represents social network and friends, the individual's connection with their peers may also be affected.

Found in the Month Pillar, this configuration signifies the individual's struggle to form an adequate connection with their parents. They may also struggle with their working relationships with their managers and colleagues, as this Pillar also represents one's career.

The relationship with their children will be affected if this configuration is seen in the Hour Pillar. As the Hour Pillar can also represent thoughts, dreams and aspirations, a position here could indicate that the individual will feel lost and uncertain about their path.

Should this configuration appear in the Luck Pillar, the individual may be confronted with a great many obstacles to their achieving success. They have many challenges to overcome and they may face disappointments. This will be a time of growth and change.

The presence of the Heaven and Earth Clash in the Annual Pillar is a warning to the Ding Mao individual to live quietly for the year. New investments and relationships are likely to end badly. They are advised to avoid, where possible, making any major changes to their lives.

Heaven Counter Earth Clash 天剋地沖
Ding Mao 丁卯 (Fire Rabbit) + Xin You 辛酉 (Metal Rooster)

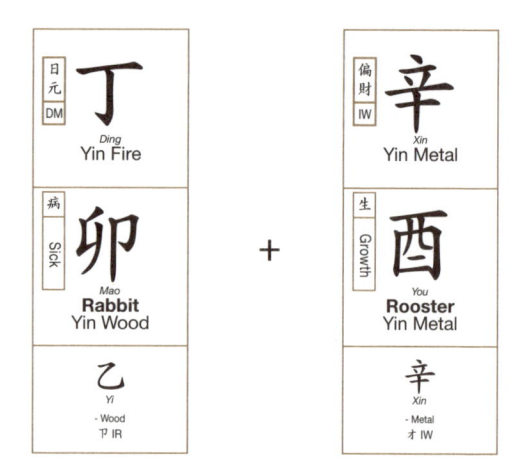

The Heaven Counter Earth Clash is an indication of passion and determination to succeed. Not to be confused with the Heaven and Earth Clash formation which acts to drain the individual's power, this configuration actually fuels their drive to achieve. Individual's with this configuration in their Chart may be impatient and even over hasty at times but they will be determined and compelled by an almost overwhelming need to win at all costs. This configuration is often associated with entrepreneurial spirit, wealth and accomplishment.

This Heaven Counter Earth Clash Pillar may appear in his BaZi Natal Chart in the Year, Month or Hour Pillars or it may emerge in the Luck and Annual Pillars.

Found in the Year Pillar of the Natal Chart, it indicates that individual will have friends with power and influence. These people will be able to help and advise the Ding Mao as they pursue their goals. It is important for this individual to not neglect to put in the hard work and avoid being too dependent on others.

134   The BaZi 60 Pillars Life Analysis Method

Should this configuration be found in the Month Pillar, the individual is likely to have a brilliant business mind. They will have a knack for turning a profit in whatever they do. However, despite their successes, they must maintain their level-headedness and not let greed get in the way.

Workaholics are more than likely have this configuration in their Hour Pillar. Their work will dominate their waking hours and they will not make time for personal relationships. They must be reminded that there is more to life than just career and business.

The appearance of this configuration in the Luck Pillar is an indication of opportunity. The individual may benefit best if they are able to take risks and grab onto every chance as it comes their way. However, they would be well advised to make sure to weigh the pros and cons before making a decision in order maximize their achievements. There is an indication here of great financial success.

If the Heaven Counter Earth Clash is located in the Annual Pillar, the individual is likely to see many opportunities for investment and advancement. They will make progress in their careers and will see an increase in their material wealth. They may need to take care of their stress levels or their personal relationships may suffer.

Heaven and Earth Unity 天同地比
Ding Mao 丁卯 (Fire Rabbit) + Ding Mao 丁卯 (Fire Rabbit)

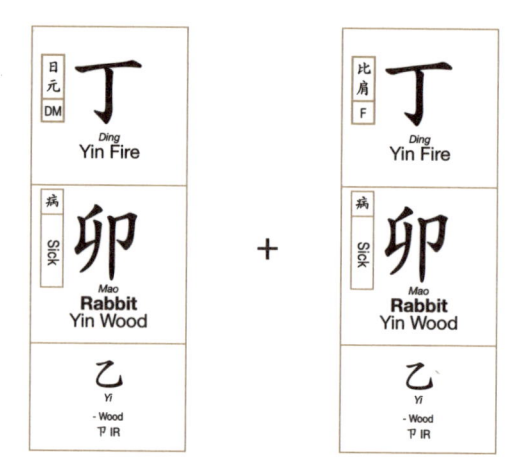

If you see another Ding Mao in the BaZi Chart this forms the Fu Yin 伏吟 formation in the Chart. It is also known as the Hidden Warning Pillar. It indicates negative emotions and sad situations or circumstances.

If this configuration appears in the Year Pillar in the Chart, it denotes a feeling of distance with regard to the grandparents and may even indicate that the individual has never met their grandparents.

When the configuration is found in the Month Pillar it suggests a feeling of distance in the individual's relationship with their parents and may struggle to connect with them on an emotional or intellectual level. This may also refer to issues of inheritance and the individual may be denied the chance to become involved in the family business.

The Hour Pillar with this configuration represents a lack of affinity with children. This may mean that the individual does not have or is unable to have children. Alternatively it could suggest that their children are being brought up in a different household.

The Heaven and Earth Unity Pillar is an indication of spirituality when it is located in the Luck Pillar. The individual is like to become very religious or alternative approaches to spirituality may become very significant to them. Alternatively they may become preoccupied with their health and fitness. Sadly this may also be an indication that they may lose a parent.

If this configuration is seen in the Annual Pillar, the individual may have something more to look forward to. They are likely to achieve a great deal in their careers and they will see a corresponding increase in their material wealth. There is the likelihood that an unhappy event will detract from their success and the gains may prove to be of little consolation.

Heaven and Earth Combo 天地相合
Ding Mao 丁卯 (Fire Rabbit) + Ren Xu 壬戌 (Water Dog)

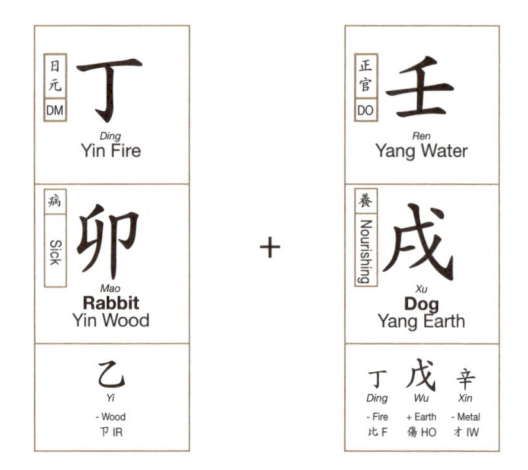

日元 DM	正官 DO
丁 Ding Yin Fire	**壬** Ren Yang Water
病 Sick	養 Nourishing
卯 Mao Rabbit Yin Wood	**戌** Xu Dog Yang Earth
乙 Yi - Wood 比 IR	丁 Ding - Fire 比 F / 戊 Wu + Earth 傷 HO / 辛 Xin - Metal 才 IW

This is the most favorable of all the Pillars. The Heaven and Earth Combine is an indication of good fortune in relationships. These relationships will have a positive impact on all areas of the Ding Mao's life making them personally happy and professionally successful.

This Pillar can also have an influence Ding Mao individuals when it is found in the Charts of individuals connected with them. These friends or colleagues are likely to be especially helpful to the Ding Mao and are likely to have a good influence on their lives.

This configuration can appear in the Year, Month and Hour Pillars as well as the Luck and Annual Pillars.

When found in the Year Pillar, it suggests that the individual will have a strong bond with their grandparents or with friends, because this individual enjoys spending quality time with them. It is also an indication of an improved social status.

When located in the Month Pillar, the individual is likely to be particularly close to their parents. Another indication is that the individual will also benefit from the regard of their employers, which could potentially lead to a steady career progression.

Ding Mao individuals are likely to have a happy and healthy relationship with their children when this configuration is in the Hour Pillar. They are also likely to enjoy the trust and respect of their employees and clients. As such, their career is expected to soar due to the good rapport.

The presence of this configuration in either the Luck or the Annual Pillars is an indication that positive and successful relationships will benefit the Ding Mao in all areas of their life. They will be close to their families and are lucky in love. They are also likely to be particularly successful in joint ventures and business partnerships.

Rob Wealth Goat Blade 劫財羊刃
Ding Mao 丁卯 (Fire Rabbit) + Bing Wu 丙午 (Earth Horse)

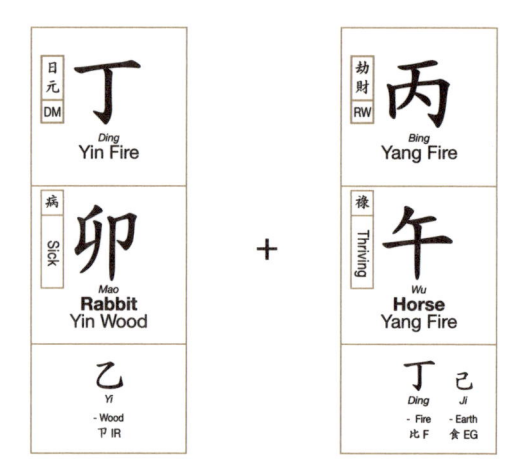

Wherever the Rob Wealth Goat Blade 劫財羊刃 appears in the Natal Chart, it is an indication of possible financial loss. When this configuration is found in the Chart of someone connected to the Ding Mao, that individual is likely to be a cause of them losing money. This may not be through any malicious intent on their part. They may be the source of poor advice or it could simply be that the Ding Mao spends more money when they are together.

丁巳

Ding Si

丁丑	丁卯	丁巳	丁未	丁酉	丁亥
Ding Chou	Ding Mao	Ding Si	Ding Wei	Ding You	Ding Hai

Getting to Know
Ding Si 丁巳 (Fire Snake)

丁巳

Ding Si

八字一柱論命法

丁巳
Fire
Snake

Positive Imagery

Negative Imagery

八字一柱論命法

丁巳
Fire Snake

The BaZi 60 Pillars Life Analysis Method 147

Getting to Know
Ding Si 丁巳 (Fire Snake)

General Observations:

Individuals born under the Ding Si Pillar are likened to the shine and glimmer of fine jewels. They may appear to be just a speck of light in a glistening sea of colour but that does not mean they are not able to shine and impress in their own right. They are often very beautiful people. Also fiercely independent and highly determined, the Ding Si individual is at their best when they are challenged and placed in the forefront, where they can display a stunning array of talent which gives them the potential to achieve great things in life.

Forward thinking, imaginative and inventive, the Ding Si individual thrives on excitement and new ideas. They will often choose the road less travelled precisely because of the challenge and inspiration that it may bring. Once their passion is engaged with a goal in mind and a task to accomplish, the Ding Si will be disciplined and perseverant, working hard and with great stamina to overcome any obstacle.

Practical, rational and precise, the Ding Si individual will often analyse all the information before coming to a logical conclusion. They have very sharp minds and are very astute, perceptive and observant, they often learn from experience and they have a spark of genius to solve problems in new and inventive ways and to innovate and improve outmoded systems. They are often to be found involved in new projects and seeking new intellectual horizons.

Flexible and adaptable, they are also very sociable with a gift for judging character. They have exceptional networking abilities and are able to mix with a wide variety of people. They are clear and precise communicators with the ability to express themselves using both wit and sensitivity. They are deeply humanitarian, understanding and perceptive. They often find their greatest successes when working with others either as part of a team or in a management capacity. They can be truly inspirational leaders. With a great need for social interaction, they enjoy a changing environment and the stimulation that new thoughts and approaches give to their own intellectual growth.

Nevertheless the Ding Si values their own individuality and they will often develop a unique approach to life even though that may be at odds with the rest of the world. They have a deep need for self-expression and can even be quite rebellious. They may be stubborn at times and they often need to work to overcome a tendency to be too strong-willed.

The Ding Si individual's biggest enemy may often be an inability to focus. They are likely to be pulled in a hundred different directions by a wide range of interests and they may be inclined to spread themselves too thin. They would be wise to cultivate a sense of purpose and focus if they are to bring their fearsome talents to bare and achieve the success they so richly deserve. Equally, while over-stimulation may lead them to become involved in too many things, boredom may produce the opposite effect and they can be given to coasting and resting on their laurels. This inertia may also be the result of indecision caused by the over-analysis of the information available and it would be wise for the Ding Si individual to develop faith in themselves and in their instincts.

Perfectionism may compel the Ding Si individual to place their standards too high and they may judge themselves and others quite harshly. They can be very sensitive and prone to depression if they are too hard on themselves. They are given to fluctuating moods and if unfulfilled, they may begin to repress their more powerful emotions and they may resort to overindulgence or fantasy as a means of escape. They have a great need for personal security and the love and affection of genuine relationships and they may need to work to keep their more playful side alive. The pursuit of spirituality and taking time for introspection and personal growth may also help them to find a greater sense of harmony and loan them faith in their natural insight.

The Ding Si individual will often be drawn to the finer things in life; they know how to enjoy themselves and to entertain others. With a great sense of dignity and an acute awareness of their public perception, they will take pains to be well presented and are likely to take an interest in fashion. They have a love of luxury and their desire for security will inspire them to build a comfortable home. This love of quality items and good living may mean that they go through bouts of money worries, these troubles are usually short lived and they often have the opportunity to make a great success of their lives. With a little forward planning and some saving for rainy days the Ding Si individual will be able to achieve substantial financial stability.

八字一柱論命法

丁巳

Fire Snake

Though they can be emotionally impulsive and restless, the Ding Si individual is also loyal and loving and they will take their domestic responsibilities seriously. Idealistic and capable of great sacrifice for those they love, they are also very compassionate and sincere and place great value on their close relationships. They may, however, need to guard against becoming too controlling or interfering too much in the lives of their loved ones and by so doing prevent them from learning and growing in their own way.

Key Character Traits of the Ding Si 丁巳: Overall

- Inventive
- Creative
- Enthusiastic
- Spiritual
- Insightful
- Social
- Original thinker
- Pragmatic

Work Life

丁巳

Ding Si

Professional Self

Precise and responsible with a great sense of determination and a competitive nature, the Ding Si will be an asset in almost any working environment. They are original thinkers often able to look outside of the box and imagine innovative solutions to complex problems. They have a shrewd business sense and a meticulous eye for detail. Naturally ambitious, they will work hard with dedication and discipline when they have a goal in mind and they will take great pride in their work.

Able communicators with a gift for psychology and a talent for charming and inspiring others, the Ding Si individual may be very well suited to working in groups or cooperative endeavors. They have a great sense of their image and public perception and they will work hard to project a professional demeanor that will make them uniquely suited to customer facing work. However as they are reluctant to take orders and are fiercely independent, they may be better suited to management positions in which they have a greater freedom to express their individuality. Their innate practicality and ability to plan gives them all the skills necessary to create method and order and to stage manage large projects. They may instead however choose to work independently and set up their own business in order to benefit from the freedom this entails.

The Ding Si individual is multitalented and they will perform best in a role where they are challenged. Boredom may lead them to become listless and they may start to underperform if their talents are not utilized so it will be vital for them to take up a career path that allows for constant change and progression.

Career Options

The Ding Si individual may be able to find success in any number of career ventures. With a deep understanding of people and exceptional communication skills, they might find success in sales, marketing or public relations and their executive abilities and hard-working perfectionism are likely to see them progress fast to management level where they will almost certainly excel. Alternatively they may choose to add their communication skills to their creativity and become writers or journalists. They also have a flair for the dramatic and an eye for beauty which could lead them to finding fulfillment through using their imaginative minds for creative expression in the visual or performance arts.

In addition to their creativity the Ding Si is also exceptionally precise and they have calm, analytical minds and outstanding problem solving abilities. They may find stimulation in research, engineering or information technology particularly if they are able to be at the forefront of new innovations. They also have a keen eye for finance and work well in banking. Alternatively their humanitarian streak may lead them to a career in caring for others and they may be successful teachers, psychologists or social workers. Politics may provide them with an outlet for their idealism if they approach it with an eye for changing the system from within. Ultimately they may find fulfillment using their inventive minds for innovation in the social sector and in pursuing the greater good.

Key Character Traits of the Ding Si 丁巳: Work life

Positive

- Responsible
- Dependable
- Good business sense
- Productive
- Versatile

Negative

- Uncompromising
- Perfectionist
- Stubborn
- Careless
- Overcritical

Love and Relationships

丁巳

Ding Si

Love

Ding Si individuals make loyal partners and have a serious attitude when it comes to finding love. They have a unique approach to romantic relationships and are willing to work hard in order to bring harmony. When they are ready to settle down, they will be generous, giving and loving to their spouse.

Stability and security are important components in their lives, which is why money and finances play a significant point when it comes to narrowing the criteria for the perfect partner. In this sense, they have the desire to be in the company of those which are more successful and independent.

Others may find it difficult to live up to the Ding Si's high expectations and be turned off by their stubbornness. At times, they may find it difficult to express themselves. For this reason, they may be inhibited from saying what they truly feel. Also, after a while he may seem cold and distant.

Acquaintances

As friends, Ding Si individuals are friendly, warm and sociable. Others love to be around them because they possess a natural quick wit and an entertaining spark. Many people want to befriend them, though they are selective in choosing the one they trust

Ding Si individuals are naturally attracted to people who share an interest in self-improvement. It is quite common for them to turn a social event into a learning session as they are always searching for intellectual stimulation. They love to gather individuals with unorthodox views to embrace new and exciting ideas. In addition, they are always looking for avenues to exchange information and knowledge.

Once Ding Si individuals befriend a person, there is no limit as to how they will help their friends. They must be careful not to overextend themselves and expend their energies too thinly. If so, they might become too involved in others people's problem to the extent of neglecting their own.

They have a tendency at times to be stubborn, calculating and secretive, which could be off-putting when they meet new people. If they want to maintain their friendship and make a good impression, they need to work hard at preventing this from occurring.

Family

The Ding Si value inner peace and harmony in their household. As such, they prefer to operate in a household that promotes a sense of blissfulness as this resonates with their preference for a quiet and harmonious environment.

They may need to find the perfect balance between their desire for family intimacy and their yearning for freedom. This freedom is vital if they want to remain in a loving relationship. In order to satisfy their freedom, they should take a little time to themselves in order re-energize and gain strength. Partners of Ding Si is advised to respect their love of freedom should they require some space alone for themselves.

Key Character Traits of the Ding Si 丁巳: Love & Relationships

- Sensitivity
- Humanitarian
- Understanding
- Caring
- Need for security

Famous Personalities

Tony Blair – British Labour Party politician who served as Prime Minister between 1997 and 2007.

Kobe Bryant - American basketball player, nicknamed the "Black Mamba", who plays for the NBA's Los Angeles Lakers.

Jennifer Aniston - American actress, film director and producer. She is best known for her role in the popular 90s television sitcom, Friends.

Kate Moss - British supermodel, mostly known for her controversial private life and relationships. She is also one of the world's top-earning models today.

Source: Wikipedia (June 2013)

丁巳
Fire Snake

八字一柱論命法

Technical Analysis

丁巳

Ding Si

BaZi Day Pillar Analytics 日柱分析

時 Hour	日 Day	月 Month	年 Year	
	日元 DM 丁 *Ding* Yin Fire			天干 Heavenly Stems
	旺 Prosperous 巳 *Si* **Snake** Yin Fire			地支 Earthly Branches
	庚 Geng + Metal 財 DW 丙 Bing + Fire 劫 RW 戊 Wu + Earth 傷 HO			藏干 Hidden Stems

丁巳

Fire Snake

Bing Fire sits in the hidden Branches of this Ding Si Pillar. As the Ding 丁 Stem is Yin Fire and the Bing 丙 is Yang Fire, this Pillar symbolizes extreme brightness and illumination of the Fire element. The Ding Si is likely to be very philosophical in nature and they may be compelled to seek enlightenment and understanding of the laws of nature. The Ding Si individual is also very compassionate with a love of helping others and this suggests that they are likely to take their learning and light the way for others to follow in their footsteps.

The Ding Si individual has a highly creative and imaginative mind. This is the effect of the hidden Eating God Star 食神星 inside the Si (Snake). They have a great sense of adventure and love the thrill of meeting new people, influenced by the Rob Wealth Star 劫財星. Always aware that there is more to be discovered, they have a restless need to be out in the world finding new experiences, with their sharp intellect and incredible versatility they are often able to make the most out of any situation they encounter.

The Ding Si may indeed find that this drive to learn and grow, to be constantly active, is the inspiration behind their greatest successes in life. Their minds are able to absorb new information and put it to practical use with incredible speed. They are self-reliant, resourceful and talented. They have natural leadership abilities and enjoy leading and starting new projects. With perception, forethought and forward planning, they have all the skills they require to follow their inspiration through from conception to tangible reality. If they have a special calling, a personal quest or a breakthrough they just have to make, they should be encouraged to see it through without allowing others to undermine their dream. All this is possible thanks to the combined influence of the hidden Rob Wealth劫財, Eating God 食神 and Direct Wealth正財 Stars.

The Ding Si person takes great pride in their work and they will do whatever it takes to ensure they achieve results in their careers They are likely to make their professional life their first priority and they will judge themselves and others by their accomplishments. If they are not happy with the direction of their lives, they would not hesitate to alter their plans and make the necessary changes. Swift at responding to a problem, they also get a deep sense of satisfaction, if not active pleasure, out of solving them.

While those around them may perceive the Ding Si as over-confident, the reality is that they often battle with secret insecurities. They may doubt their own abilities and can be easily discouraged by other people. Privately they may struggle with feelings of anxiety and they have a deep need for support and recognition.

These disparate sides to their personality can make them changeable and although they may be idealistic and sensitive, they can also be inconsiderate and unfair in the heat of the moment. They may find that learning to trust their intuition will help them to find a more balanced approach to dealing with others and a calmer inner world.

Technical Observations

The Ding Si 丁巳 sits on a Traveling Star, which, as you may guess, indicates frequent travel and mobility. The Ding Fire stem here, is considered one of the dimmest of all the Ding Stems since the Ding Si Pillar is sitting on the Rob Wealth Star 劫財星. In essence, it is the Bing 丙 sunlight fire in the Hidden Stem that is outshining the Ding 丁 candle. This signifies potential for the Ding Si to contend with some inner turmoil and it may explain why they are so competitive in nature, always striving to gain the upper hand and prove themselves.

Should the Ji Si 己巳, Bing Wu 丙午 or Ding Wei 丁未 Hour Pillars be present in the Ding Si's BaZi Chart it is a favorable sign. With these formations the Ding Si individual is likely to find that success and fulfillment come easily for them. This is because these Pillars strengthen the quality of the Ding Fire over Bing Fire, indicating victory over the self and good control over their inner conflicts. It should be noted that the Ding Si's biggest enemy, or competitor, is always themselves, conquering their emotions is often the key to the Ding Si finding ultimate success in life.

It is also favourable when this Pillar meets with the Wood 木, Fire 火 and Earth 土 elements in the Luck Pillars. Similarly, these elements also help to preserve and enhance the brightness of the Ding Fire against the overwhelming power of the Bing Fire. These elements in the luck cycle suggest a period of good fortune and happiness. It is likely that there will be unfavourable indications, however, if this Pillar meets with excessive Metal and Water elements in the Luck Pillars. In this situation the Ding Fire will not have enough energy to control the Metal or to withstand the Water and they may find that they face a period of trials and tribulations.

The Si 巳 (Snake) is the Growth Position 長生 (12 Birth and Growth Phases of BaZi) of Geng 庚 Metal, the Direct Wealth Star 正財星. If the Geng Metal appears in the Stems it is an indication of a successful professional life. If the Geng Metal does not appear on the Stems, the Ding Si's is likely to find that they will become wealthy through working partnerships and with the help and support of others. This is because the Wealth Star is positioned together with a Rob Wealth 劫財星, a companion star.

There may be good luck in store, including prosperity, for the Ding Si born in the Spring and Summer months. Those born in the Winter and Autumn months, meanwhile, will benefit from a sharp business sense and they are likely to achieve success by their own business. The Ding Si born during the day time (5AM – 5PM) can expect to meet with good fortune through various investments or business endeavors. Those born at night (5PM – 5AM) can also look forward to a life of happiness and fulfillment. It is not auspicious for a Ding Si person to be born in the Wei 未 (Goat) month, as they will experience a fluctuation of wealth during their lifetime.

Unique 60 Pillar Combinations

This section covers the relationships between the individual pillar under this elemental polarity and several other pillars found in the 60 Jia Zi cycle.

丁巳

Ding Si

Heaven Combine Earth Punish 天合地刑
Ding Si 丁巳 (Fire Snake) + Ren Shen 壬申 (Water Monkey)

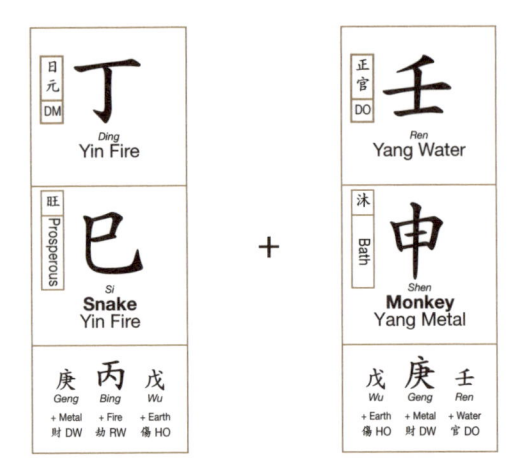

日元 DM — **Ding** Yin Fire 丁	正官 DO — **Ren** Yang Water 壬
旺 Prosperous — **Si** Snake Yin Fire 巳	沐 Bath — **Shen** Monkey Yang Metal 申
庚 Geng +Metal 財 DW / 丙 Bing +Fire 劫 RW / 戊 Wu +Earth 傷 HO	戊 Wu +Earth 傷 HO / 庚 Geng +Metal 財 DW / 壬 Ren +Water 官 DO

This Pillar combines at the Heavenly Stem to form a Punishment with the Earthly Branch. The Heavenly Stem would appear to be a positive indication but the Punishment formation often manifests as emotional pain. The indications are that, seen through the public eye, this individual will appear to be very happy but they will be carrying unhappiness and tension in their heart. This configuration is also known as the Heaven Combine Earth Combine formation, depending on the overall BaZi Chart. Some configurations would have the positive formation of the Heaven Combine Earth Combine to become more apparent, while others would favor the manifestation of the Heaven and Earth Punish.

This Heaven Combine Earth Punish configuration can be found in the BaZi Natal Chart of a Ding Si person in their Year, Month, and Hour Pillars and also in the Luck and Annual Pillars.

Should this configuration be located in the Year Pillar, it is likely that beneath the façade of an amicable relationship with the individual's grandparents there will be much hidden tension and discord.

Found in the Month Pillar, the individual may appear to be very close with their parents but there will be turbulent emotions hidden beneath the surface. If the Heaven Combine Earth Punish is seen in the Month Pillar, it can also affect the Ding Si individual's working relationships. Though the individual may appear to benefit from a pleasant professional environment and positive connections with their colleagues and supervisors they will nevertheless be uncomfortable with the office dynamic. They may be stressed and feel that office politics is to blame. However the source of the problem is likely to reside within themselves and they will only be able to overcome these issues when they resolve their own emotions.

When this configuration is found in the Hour Pillar, the individual is likely to over-extend themselves. They may fail to deliver on their promises. It is likely that they are so eager to please that they struggle to decline a request even when they know they do n ot have the time to fulfill it. They will unwittingly cause some ill feeling if they do not learn to only take on the tasks they know they can complete.

Should this arrangement be found in the Luck Pillar, the individual may lack faith in their own abilities during this cycle. They are likely to be successful and admired but they will feel unworthy of their good fortune and if they do not work to overcome their low self-esteem they may find that they sabotage their own potential.

When found in the Annual Pillar, the Heaven Combine Earth Punish indicates a difficult year in which plans will go astray and the individual is likely to be insecure about their relationships and fear they are not trusted. They need to work to remain calm during this time. It is quite possible that their own negativity is the source of their problems.

Heaven Combine Earth Harm 天合地害
Ding Si 丁巳 (Fire Snake) + Ren Yin 壬寅 (Water Tiger)

日元 DM	丁 Ding Yin Fire
旺 Prosperous	巳 Si Snake Yin Fire

庚 Geng	丙 Bing	戊 Wu
+ Metal 財 DW	+ Fire 劫 RW	+ Earth 傷 HO

+

正官 DO	壬 Ren Yang Water
死 Death	寅 Yin Tiger Yang Wood

戊 Wu	甲 Jia	丙 Bing
+ Earth 傷 HO	+ Wood 印 DR	+ Fire 劫 RW

This Pillar combines with the Heavenly Stem to form a Harm 害 with the Earthly Branch. The outward indications of this configuration would appear to be excellent due to the presence of the Heavenly Stem but the Harm indicates that the individual's true feelings will be far less settled. There are indications here of uncertainty, confusion and distrust.

This combination is found in the BaZi Natal Chart in the Year, Month and Hour Pillars as well as the Luck and Annual Pillars.

Located in the Year Pillar, the individual is likely to be uncertain about their relationship with their grandparents and friends. The relationship may appear to be positive but it will not be entirely secure, as hidden tensions are bubbling under the surface.

Similarly, should this configuration be located in the Month Pillar, the Ding Si individual and their parents may seem to enjoy a good relationship but there will be hidden tensions and there may be some issues of trust and loyalty to be contended with. These feelings may also extend to the individual's working relationships as the Month Pillar also governs career.

Should this formation be located in the Hour Pillar, these concerns may be reflected in their feelings about their children or about their clients and customers. The individual may feel that they do not have the respect and appreciation of these individuals.

Located in the Luck Pillar, this configuration is likely to indicate that apparent success will fail to bring peace of mind during this period. The individual is likely to achieve a great deal but they will believe that this has come at a high personal cost. They are likely to be left feeling exhausted and even abused in some way.

The presence of this configuration in the Annual Pillar suggests that the year will show great promise but may end in frustration and disillusionment. The individual may need to review their own thoughts and recognize that jealousy is distorting their perception of their own achievements. They should have more faith in themselves.

Heaven Friend Earth Clash 天比地沖
Ding Si 丁巳 (Fire Snake) + Ding Hai 丁亥 (Fire Pig)

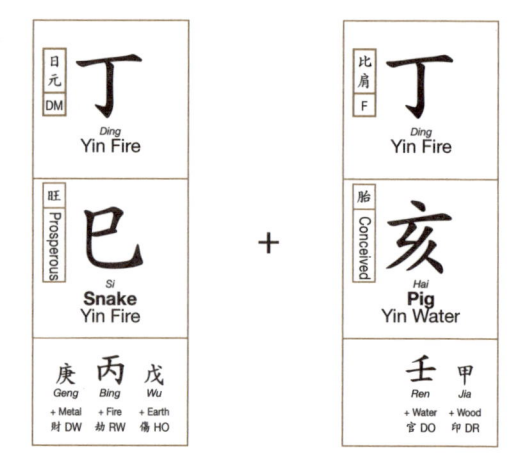

日元 DM		比肩 F	
丁 Ding Yin Fire		**丁** Ding Yin Fire	
旺 Prosperous	**巳** Si Snake Yin Fire	胎 Conceived	**亥** Hai Pig Yin Water
庚 Geng +Metal 財 DW	丙 Bing +Fire 劫 RW	戊 Wu +Earth 傷 HO	壬 Ren +Water 官 DO	甲 Jia +Wood 印 DR

This configuration often represents unexpected events or situations. An agreement made in good faith may eventually fall apart, events are unlikely to unfold as anticipated and plans may not have the desired outcome. The individual is likely to feel unhappy and disappointed. The ultimate conclusion may yet prove to be a positive however depending on the Heavenly Stem. The individual is also likely to find that they are very busy but their efforts may fail to result in any material achievements.

This combination can be found in the BaZi Natal Chart in the Year, Month or Hour Pillars. It can also appear in the Luck Pillars and the Annual Pillar.

Should it appear in the Year, Month or Hour Pillars of the Natal Chart, the individual will feel these effects in their relationships with the parties represented by each Pillar.

If found in the Year Pillar, this configuration indicates a feeling of dissatisfaction and discontent with one's grandparents or even friendships.

In the Month Pillar, the impact will be felt in the relationship the individual has with their parents or guardian. They are likely to face some turbulence and disagreements in these connections. As the Month Pillar also has a bearing on career or business, a placement in this Pillar can additionally suggest that the same emotions will be felt in working relationships, specifically with colleagues and superiors.

In the Hour Pillar, the individual's relationship with their children will be the one most affected. A placement here in the Hour Pillar may also have an impact on their dreams, hopes and aspirations. The individual may experience may feel that they are unable to achieve all that they hope for or they may lack for direction and a sense of purpose. Alternatively it may be their ideas and contributions that are affected. A potentially good idea may fail in the implementation and unexpected new ideas may rush in to take its place. The individual may find their feeling of making a valid contribution to the world is shaken.

A period of steady change can be expected when this configuration is found in the Luck Pillar. This may not appear to be a positive time, it may even be painful, but the individual will ultimately benefit from real growth and progression.

If the Heaven Friend Earth Clash is found in the Annual Pillar, the individual is likely to experience a year of turbulent twists and turns. They will have to work their way through some personal struggles but they will learn a great deal about themselves and be enriched by the experience.

Heaven and Earth Clash 天沖地沖
Ding Si 丁巳 (Fire Snake) + Gui Hai 癸亥 (Water Pig)

日元 DM	丁 Ding Yin Fire		七殺 7K	癸 Gui Yin Water
旺 Prosperous	巳 Si Snake Yin Fire	+	胎 Conceived	亥 Hai Pig Yin Water

Hidden stems under 巳: 庚 Geng +Metal 財 DW, 丙 Bing +Fire 劫 RW, 戊 Wu +Earth 傷 HO

Hidden stems under 亥: 壬 Ren +Water 官 DO, 甲 Jia +Wood 印 DR

The Heaven and Earth Clash Pillar is a configuration in which the Day Pillar is clashed by the Gui Hai Pillar. This is known as the Fan Yin 反吟 and it has the effect of diminishing the good qualities of an individual's Day Pillar. This Pillar impairs the individual's chances of success. It is also recommended for the Ding Si to seek out this formation in the Chart of those connected to them. Those with this formation in the Chart may prove to be negative influence on the Ding Si, even though they may be perfectly pleasant people.

Found in the Hour, Day Month or Year Pillar of the Ding Si's Natal Chart, this configuration indicates that the individuals will have a weak or negative relationship with the person or persons indicated by that particular Pillar.

If this combination is seen the Year Pillar, the individual's relationship with their grandparents may be quite poor. Alternatively they may find that they struggle in their social circles and they may find it hard to make friends.

Where this combination is found in the Month Pillar, the individual's relationship with their parents will feel the effects and they are find it exceptionally difficult to develop a positive bond with them. As the Month Pillar also denotes career and business, the individual may also need to be particularly careful in how they deal with their managers and colleagues as these relationships may be prone to difficulty.

In the Hour Pillar, the strained relationship is likely to be between the individual and their children or employees. The appearance of this configuration in the Hour Pillar can also represent the individual's ability to fulfil their hopes and dreams and they may have to work harder than their peers to achieve all that they set out for.

Located in the Luck Pillar, this configuration denotes a period in which the individual may find that they are forced to contend with a series of obstacles and challenges. In the face of these difficult times the individual is advised to stay perseverant and optimistic. They should try to have faith in the knowledge that through adversity comes strength and experience.

If the Heaven and Earth Clash appears in the Annual Pillar, the individual is advised to delay their important decisions at least for this year. In other words, they should keep a low profile and avoid making any major changes to their lives.

Heaven Counter Earth Clash 天剋地沖
Ding Si 丁巳 (Fire Snake) + Xin Hai 辛亥 (Metal Pig)

日元 DM	丁 Ding Yin Fire
旺 Prosperous	巳 Si Snake Yin Fire

| 庚 Geng + Metal 財 DW | 丙 Bing + Fire 劫 RW | 戊 Wu + Earth 傷 HO |

+

偏財 IW	辛 Xin Yin Metal
胎 Conceived	亥 Hai Pig Yin Water

| 壬 Ren + Water 官 DO | 甲 Jia + Wood 印 DR |

Unlike the Heaven and Earth Clash which acts to drain a Pillar of its positive qualities, the Heaven Counter Earth Clash may be able to work in their favor. This configuration gives the individual a burning desire to be in control and to win at all costs. These individuals are likely to be dominant personalities with good business sense. Though they may, at times, appear to be impatient or over hasty, their determination may lead them to great achievements. This Pillar is often considered to be an indication of wealth and success.

This arrangement can be found in the BaZi Natal Chart in the Year, Month, and Hour Pillars as well as Luck and Annual Pillars.

When found in the Year Pillar, the individual may find that they are surrounded by wealthy and influential friends who are willing and able to offer help and advice. This individual should remember to show their appreciation for the help they receive and they should not become complaisant or overly reliant on the support of others. They will need to remember that they will still have to work to in order to earn their success.

When this arrangement is located in the Month Pillar, the individual is likely to be endowed with exceptional entrepreneurial instincts and they will take great satisfaction in their financial successes. This individual must guard against allowing greed to color their judgment.

Appearing in the Hour Pillar, the individual is likely to prioritize their career above all else, they will work all hours they have available and will not find time for their families or personal relationships. This individual needs to learn how to maintain a balance in life, as not everything in life revolves around work.

When found in the Luck Pillar, the individual is likely to find their career success results in great financial returns. In the face of this, the individual is advised to remain level-headed and humble, and not to allow themselves to become too money-minded or materialistic.

Should this configuration be found in the Annual Pillar, the individual will benefit from a series of great opportunities for investment and career progression. They may become involved in new ventures or new working partnerships. They may find that they are placed under a fair amount of pressure and their personal relationships may feel the strain.

Heaven and Earth Unity 天同地比
Ding Si 丁巳 (Fire Snake) + Ding Si 丁巳 (Fire Snake)

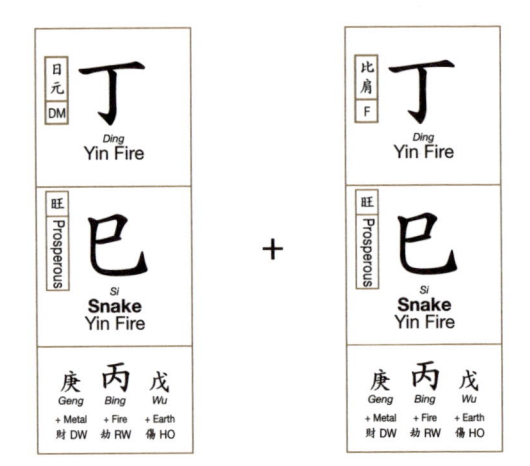

Also called the Hidden Warning Pillar or the Fu Yin 伏吟 formation, this configuration is an indication of sorrowful events. This Heaven and Earth Unity may appear in the Year, Month or Hour Pillars as well as the Luck Pillar and the Annual Pillar of the BaZi Natal Chart.

When found in the Year Pillar, the implication is that the individual will have only a weak connection with their grandparents. It may even mean they have never had the opportunity to know them. As the Year Pillar also signifies friends and social circles it may be that the individual is inclined to feeling lonely and isolated from time to time.

The appearance of the Heaven and Earth Unity in the Month Pillar, may suggest that the individual is not close to their parents. They may struggle to connect with them on a deeper emotional level. Alternatively this position may indicate that they are unable to inherit or that they miss out on an opportunity to become involved in the family business. A position here may also impact upon the individual's career and it could be that they struggle to be able to progress or to form positive relationships with their colleagues and superiors.

Should this configuration be present in the Hour Pillar, the individual may not have the close relationship with their children that they desire. They may have been separated from their children or rarely have the opportunity to spend quality time with them due to other circumstances. Alternatively, it may be that they do not have children or they find that they are unable to have children. As the Hour Pillar also connects to hopes and aspirations it is possible that the individual may struggle to be able to turn their dreams into reality.

When located in the Luck Pillar, this configuration symbolizes spiritual development during this period. The individual may choose to follow a religious vocation or they may study theology. Alternatively they may become very focused on their health. Sadly it may also represent the loss of a parent.

In the Annual Pillar, this formation is often an indication of achievement. The individual may progress in their careers, acquire new property or see an increase in their material wealth. The year may be marred by at least one distressing event.

Heaven and Earth Combo 天地相合
Ding Si 丁巳 (Fire Snake) + Ren Yin 壬寅 (Water Tiger)

丁 Ding — Yin Fire (日元 DM)
巳 Si Snake — Yin Fire (旺 Prosperous)
  - 庚 Geng + Metal 財 DW
  - 丙 Bing + Fire 劫 RW
  - 戊 Wu + Earth 傷 HO

+

壬 Ren — Yang Water (正官 DO)
申 Shen Monkey — Yang Metal (沐 Bath)
  - 戊 Wu + Earth 傷 HO
  - 庚 Geng + Metal 財 DW
  - 壬 Ren + Water 官 DO

The Heaven and Earth Combine is the luckiest of all the possible configurations. It indicates strong, healthy and happy relationships with friends, family and loved ones. These individuals are also likely to benefit from positive business connections that help them to become successful. This is also known as the Heaven Combine Earth Punish 天合地刑 formation, depending on the overall configuration of the Chart. Some configurations would enable more of the negative formation (Heaven Combine Earth Punish) to surface, while some would favor the manifestation of the Heaven and Earth Combine.

This Pillar may also have a beneficial effect when seen in the BaZi Charts of those connected to the Ding Si individual. These people will be a good influence and they will offer help and support in times of need. This is of course, assuming that the Chart leans towards the formation of the Heaven and Earth Combine instead of the Heaven and Earth Punish configuration.

182 The BaZi 60 Pillars Life Analysis Method

This configuration can be present in the BaZi Chart of others in the Year, Month and Hour Pillars as well as the Luck and Annual Pillars.

Should the combination lie in the Year Pillar, the Ding Si individual is likely to have a very good relationship with their grandparents. The Year Pillar also connects to their social circles and it is likely that they will enjoy popularity with their friends and a good social status.

When seen in the Month Pillar, this configuration represents an excellent and harmonious bond with parents. Since the Month Pillar also represents career it denotes a strong relationship with employers.

When this configuration happens in the Hour Pillar, the Ding Si will maintain a deep and loving relationship with their children whether those children be biological their own or adopted. They will also be respected and trusted by clients and employees.

Located in either the Luck or Annual Pillars, the Heaven and Earth Combine is an indication that the Ding Si individual will enjoy the benefits of positive relationships in all areas of their life. They are likely to be close to their families, lucky in love and involved in successful business partnerships.

Rob Wealth Goat Blade 劫財羊刃
Ding Si 丁巳 (Fire Snake) + Bing Wu 丙午 (Fire Horse)

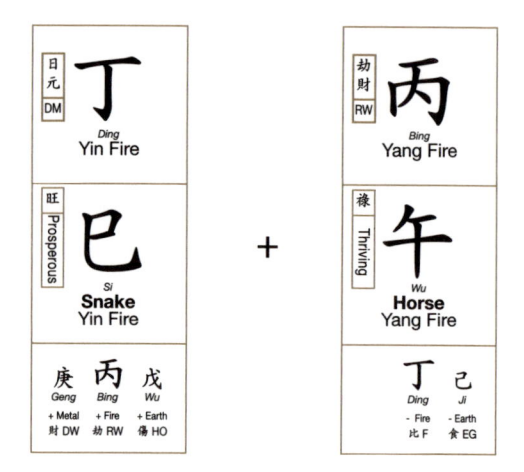

日元 DM	劫財 RW
丁 Ding Yin Fire	丙 Bing Yang Fire
旺 Prosperous 巳 Si Snake Yin Fire	祿 Thriving 午 Wu Horse Yang Fire
庚 Geng + Metal 財 DW / 丙 Bing + Fire 劫 RW / 戊 Wu + Earth 傷 HO	丁 Ding - Fire 比 F / 己 Ji - Earth 食 EG

The Rob Wealth Goat Blade 劫財羊刃 Pillar has the effect of draining the individual's resources. Whether it is found in their own Chart or in the Chart of someone connected to them, the effect will be very much the same and will result in the same negative outcome.

If this configuration is found in the Charts of individuals connected to the Ding Si, these people may cause them to lose money. It is an unlikely to be a deliberate or malicious attempt, it may simply be that Ding Si spends more when they are together and they may be quite happy to do so.

丁未

Ding Wei

丁丑	丁卯	丁巳	丁未	丁酉	丁亥
Ding Chou	Ding Mao	Ding Si	Ding Wei	Ding You	Ding Hai

Getting to Know
Ding Wei 丁未 (Fire Goat)

丁未

Ding Wei

Positive Imagery

丁未
Fire Goat

190 The BaZi 60 Pillars Life Analysis Method

Negative Imagery

丁未

Fire Goat

Getting to Know
Ding Wei 丁未 (Fire Goat)

General Observations:

The crackle of a burning fire captures the essence of those born under the Ding Wei 丁未 Pillar. This reflects the gregarious, spontaneous and outgoing nature of these individuals.

Ding Wei individuals are zealous, dynamic, determined, energetic and idealistic. They are brilliantly intelligent, and possess a commanding personality full of vitality and energy. Endowed with an inherent joy for life, they have a perpetual youthful quality.

It is not unusual for Ding Wei individuals to show signs of artistic talent. In addition, they may also display spiritual and psychic ability. It is through these traits they find ways to express their originality. Ding Wei individuals are also gourmands who have exquisite tastes in good food, and are more inclined to the arts and philosophy.

They have a flair for fame and wealth and are excellent at managing their money. These qualities provide them the opportunity to do many things without worry, which is why they believe that nothing is impossible.

Even though there are few obstacles standing in the way of Ding Wei individuals' success, the key for them is to focus on one goal at a time. This allows them to focus their energies where needed and discover the sweetness associated with great success. Lofty dreams materialize when they concentrate on diligence and hard work.

It helps that the Ding Wei are fast learners. They can absorb knowledge quickly, although in their case, it mostly applied to practical or hands-on matters. As such, you might not find them poring through piles of books, or researching through written materials for ways to improve their ability. Rather, they are accustomed to learn by observation, doing and they master their craft through practice.

Gifted with the talent to work with tools, they are all-rounded handyman who loves to make things the D-I-Y way or simply improve the functionality, where they see fit. In this sense, they are also amazed by the intricacies of science or gadgets and it drives to them acquire knowledge and experience in these fields. Many Ding Weis are attracted to high-tech tools such as technology, weaponry, computers or cameras.

The only way in which they can utilize their full creative potential is to know exactly what they want. Ding Wei spend the early part of their life searching for their life purpose. Most will only discover this by mid life. Life fulfillment can be achieved. They will do this by creating and maintaining a clear vision of their goals. Then they need to methodically plan for their manifestation.

Around their friends, they are known to be the go-to person because the Ding Wei have caring and giving nature. They are accustomed to helping others. Naturally helpful, they have many friends who appreciate this trait in them and who enjoy their company.

八字一柱論命法

丁未
Fire Goat

The Ding Wei wouldn't miss any invitation to the latest or most happening social gathering as they are seen as the light of the party. Their joyful nature is infectious and they enjoy being around people, with the feeling being mutual.

Like the crackle of a burning fire, the Ding Wei is noisier and more talkative than many individuals. They excel in the art of sarcasm and dry humor, and love to surround themselves with others just like them. In a nutshell, they have eloquence sprinkled liberally throughout their speech.

In addition, they must guard against their innate restlessness. If they do not get their way, they can turn moody and overbearing. This is when many will see their stormy temper.

In their moments of unhappiness or despair, they may want to "hide their heads in the sand". This shows their tendency to want to escape or wallow in self-pity. They can actually avoid much of this by trusting their powerful instincts. This way, they can take advantage of these unexpected events, instead of reacting negatively to them.

Although traditionally fruitful in the area of money, those of this Pillar are not as lucky when it comes to producing children. It may take quite a while for them to be able to actually bear a child. Once they finally have children, their relationships may very well be strained and tenuous.

Key Character Traits of the Ding Wei 丁未: Overall

- Commanding
- Personable
- Determined
- Creative
- Intuitive
- Witty
- Funny
- Talkative

丁未
Fire
Goat

Work Life

丁未

Ding Wei

Professional Self

It is not always easy to predict exactly the precise profession or career the Ding Wei will take. Their innate love of travel and change causes them to experiment with a variety of occupations. When they do take up a career, they are loyal and dedicated.

They enjoy initiating projects and are continuously searching for ways to use their bright intellect. They fully embrace the idea of thinking big, which is why they are perfect for starting their own business. Always hardworking, they throw themselves into a project they sincerely love and dedicate themselves until completion.

Their forthright style and dynamic approach to solving problems makes them an asset to any firm. These traits virtually guarantee that they will not squander their time, but instead go directly to their goals and achieve it. They are indeed extremely ambitious and have strong desires on where they want to go. They also are endowed with magnificent leadership skills.

Their natural flair for the arts may pull them into careers involving music, painting, photography, drama or even martial arts. This also satisfies their desire to surround themselves with glory, victory, beauty, style and luxury.

Any craft that requires skills with hands is desired by the Ding Wei, particularly because they are good at it. Handicraft, sculpting, carpentry or professions involving the need and use of high-tech gadgetry work will do well to challenge them and keeping them inspired.

The Ding Wei also carries a Medical Star 天醫 in its Pillar, indicating superior talent in the healing arts such as physiotherapy, meridian pressure point treatments, acupuncture, acupressure, massage and posture alignment. Given enough time and practice, they can further their knowledge in these fields and master the art proficiently.

The Ding Wei communicates well and understands the importance of values. These traits, along with their leadership skills, will make them perfect for any position of authority, regardless of the field.

Career Options

Between their ambition, intuitiveness and outspoken nature, Ding Wei individuals are suitable for a plethora of careers.

Their love for information and knowledge, combined with their ability to fuel enthusiasm in others, would make them ideal coaches and trainers.

Their performing and entertaining traits can easily serve them well in successful careers as writers, artists, musicians or actors. Since they have grace and love physical challenges, they will do well in sports and in martial arts.

If these individuals decide that they want to become a negotiator, success is assured due to their intuitive understanding of people and outspoken instincts on behalf of others. Their natural ability to understand others actually pushes them into the role of either a formal or informal advisor. This ability, along with people skills, would make them successful psychologists, therapists or counselors.

They work best when given a worthy cause, which is why Ding Wei individuals should consider becoming a spokesperson for a charity or non-profit project. They could also consider careers related to social reform or childcare. Their generous nature makes them a perfect fit for any of these positions.

Ding Wei individuals are drawn to the business field and would excel as organizers, leaders, managers or supervisors. They are not extremely adept to following orders, so becoming an entrepreneur may be best for them. They do enjoy, however, wielding power and would prefer being the individual delegating duties to others.

With their intuitive ability to sense opportunities in business, they could be successful in the fields of sales, real-estate, media, advertising, promotions or public relations.

They should be careful before they assume any position in sales, however. If they are not convinced of the product, they are not very likely to convince others either. In turn, their chances of excelling are slim.

Key Character Traits of the Ding Wei 丁未: Work life

Positive

- Ambitious
- Diplomatic
- Creative
- Pragmatic
- Enthusiastic

Negative

- Indecisive
- Temperamental
- Procrastinator
- Impulsive

八字一柱論命法

丁未

Fire Goat

Love and Relationships

丁未

Ding Wei

Love

They are sensitive romantics with powerful emotions and high aspirations. They would like nothing better than to experience a simple life with a loyal partner who stimulates them intellectually. They work diligently to find their true soul-mate and will fall head-over-heals in love. Once they find the one, they will remain loyal to them no matter what.

When it comes to the affairs of the heart, they are less than sure of themselves. They sometimes are not sure how they feel or who they love, which often leaves them feeling insecure. They find it difficult to discover a person who lives up to their expectations. If their partner does not live up to their romanticized, lofty ideals, they can easily get frustrated. Because of this, many of their relationships are often platonic instead of romantic.

Acquaintances

Ding Wei individuals are charismatic, charming, and warm. For this reason, they have little trouble attracting a variety of friends and admirers. They are very popular due to their generosity, social savviness and interesting conversation style.

Generally, they prefer to surround themselves with people who are as hardworking and successful as they are. Always interested in their own self-improvement, they often seek out others who are clever and self-aware.

Being inherently compassionate, they are more than willing to make sacrifices for their friends. At the same time, they expect the same amount of loyalty and sacrifice from others.

Loyal and supportive themselves, they may be prone to playing the martyr and should maintain a sense of detachment.

Family

Individuals born under this Pillar are emotionally supportive of their family – whether financially or emotionally. Usually they feel the need to provide and show their love and care for others under one roof. They are a positive influence on others and usually do not recognize it.

They normally have good spousal relationships, but need to find that delicate balance between commitment and independence. Once they develop a balance, they can show their love more generously.

At times, they may become jealous towards their spouse. They should avoid this because it will destroy their loving family base. Learn to be happy for the success of others, especially if that person is your loved ones.

Key Character Traits of the Ding Wei 丁未: Love & Relationships

- Idealistic
- Loyal
- Charismatic
- Generous
- Kind
- Sociable

Famous Personalities

John DeJoria - American billionaire, businessman and philanthropist. He is the co-founder of the Paul Mitchell hair care products and the Patron Spirits Company.

David Koch - American businessman, philanthropist, political activist and chemical engineer. He is the co-founder of Koch Industries.

Judith Sheindlin - American judge, lawyer, TV personality and author. She is best known as "Judge Judy" based on her award-winning reality courtroom television series.

Serena Williams - American tennis player. She is the world's No. 1 in women's singles tennis, and is regarded as one of the greatest tennis players of all time.

Source: Wikipedia (June 2013)

Technical Analysis

丁未

Ding Wei

BaZi Day Pillar Analytics 日柱分析

時 Hour	日 Day	月 Month	年 Year	
	日元 DM **丁** Ding Yin Fire			天干 Heavenly Stems
	冠 Youth **未** Wei Goat Yin Earth			地支 Earthly Branches
	乙 Yi - Wood 乛 IR 己 Ji - Earth 食 EG 丁 Ding - Fire 比 F			藏干 Hidden Stems

丁未 Fire Goat

The Ding Wei 丁未 Pillar is seated on the Fire Storage 庫 and Rooted 通根 in the Branch. This Pillar also sits on the prosperous Eating God Star 食神星, denoting beauty, elegance, a street-savvy stride and the love of good food. This also indicates that the female Ding Wei is likely to be a virtuous wife.

The Ding Wei individual is an independent thinker. Though they are traditional at heart, they are not afraid to develop their own personal philosophy and they like to make their own rules. Often able to impress and inspire others with their original ideas and innovative approaches, they are inquisitive, adaptable and naturally gifted with words and communication.

The Ding Wei have a deep need for creative self-expression. It is likely that they will benefit greatly from using their creativity toward a practical end, in pursuit of their goals and ambitions. They desire material success

The BaZi 60 Pillars Life Analysis Method   **209**

and stability more than anything else. As they are resourceful and industrious, they should be able to build a solid foundation to turn their inspiration into tangible accomplishments. They have sound business sense and can be perfectionists when they have a target in mind.

For all their need for stability the Ding Wei can also be restless due to the combined effect of hidden Indirect Resource 偏印 and the Friend 比肩 Stars. They are very energetic and they may seem to be quite detached and irresponsible at times as they usually come and go as they please. Individuals of this Pillar are often very fun loving and they are attracted to travel and new experiences. They may have to work to develop the discipline and perseverance they need to turn their dreams into reality.

The Ding Wei individual is warm, fun and sincere. Gregarious and outgoing, they love to be involved in group activities. At their best they can radiate a true joy in life and they will be able to use their sensitivity and intuition to offer help and support to their loved ones.

When they are feeling negative however they will become insecure. They are likely to struggle with criticism. They may be overly dependent on friends and family and even become quite controlling of their environment and the people in it. They may also be shy and reserved and anxious to take part in the travels and adventures upon which they would thrive.

Technical Observations

The Ding Wei 丁未 Pillar sits on the Resource Star 印星 and is Rooted 通根 in the Branch. This is indicative of general good health, vitality and longevity. The Fire 火 element burns the Earth 土 and the Earth in turn is infused with the heat from the Fire. While this combination creates smoke, it does not produce any dangerous flames. This seemingly weak Fire can endure for a very long time. This suggests an individual with extraordinary staying power, perseverance and strong will. Since the Earth element is the Eating God Star 食神星 this indicates that the individual is intelligent, but may be arrogant and secretive.

This BaZi Chart is likely to be a good one as long as it does not Clash 沖 with the Chou 丑 (Ox). If ever a Chou 丑(Ox) is found in the Chart, it is an indication that the Ding Wei man will be countered or bullied by his wife, and that she may even act impair his chances of achievement.

It is favorable if the Ding Wei Pillar meets with additional Metal 金, Water 水 and Wood 木 elements in the Luck Pillar, as this is indicative of greater chances for financial and personal success. It is however, unfavourable for this Pillar to be overwhelmed by excessive Fire 火 and Earth 土 elements in the Luck Pillar. This is likely to indicate that the Chart will be overly dry and hot, this creates an image of drought and famine where life is destroyed be excessive heat.

The Yi 乙 Wood in this Pillar is in the Spouse Palace, which places emphasis on the Ding Wei's familial inclinations. In the study of BaZi, it is unfavorable when the Water element is contaminated by the Earth. In this situation, the Water cannot be contaminated since the Yi Wood acts as a filter, making it clear, this indirectly strengthening the chart overall. This indicates that the spouse is very helpful to this individual.

Ding Wei individuals tend not to be as wealthy as those born with the Ding Chou 丁丑 Pillar simply because the Chou 丑 (Ox) represents a gold chest. It may also be difficult for the Ding Wei to save money, as none of the three harmony of this Pillar (Pig - Rabbit-Goat) 亥卯未 formation contain any Wealth 財星 Stars. The Ding Wei may be equipped to make money but they will tend to spend it just as fast. Ding Wei individuals would be advised to work up a budget and an investment plan if they are to ensure long-term financial growth and stability.

Those who are born in the Spring and Summer months have a greater chance to find success if they are able to be frugal and diligent. Those individuals born in the Winter and Autumn months are likely to establish their own business. Should they be born in the day time (5AM – 5PM), they have the potential to suffer from lingering health challenges after the age of forty. Born at night (5PM – 5AM), they are more likely to enjoy the good life in their older years. It is less favourable to be born in the Chou 丑(Ox) month, as this is a clash month, indicating a life full of obstacles and challenges.

Unique 60 Pillar Combinations

This section covers the relationships between the individual pillar under this elemental polarity and several other pillars found in the 60 Jia Zi cycle.

丁未

Ding Wei

Heaven Combine Earth Punish 天合地刑
Ding Wei 丁未 (Fire Goat) + Ren Xu 壬戌 (Water Dog)

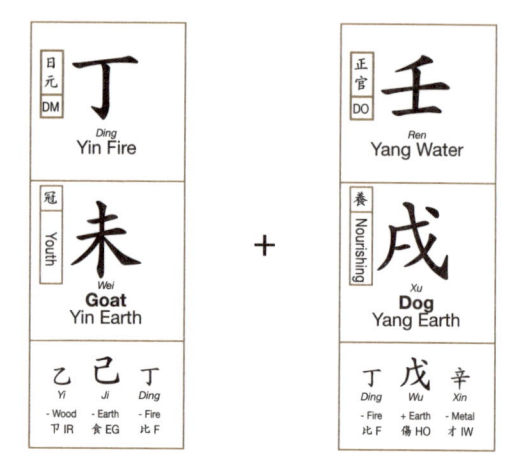

日元 DM	Ding 丁 Yin Fire
冠 Youth	Wei 未 Goat Yin Earth

	Yi - Wood 乙 甲 IR	Ji - Earth 己 食 EG	Ding - Fire 丁 比 F

正官 DO	Ren 壬 Yang Water
養 Nourishing	Xu 戌 Dog Yang Earth

	Ding - Fire 丁 比 F	Wu + Earth 戊 傷 HO	Xin - Metal 辛 才 IW

Combining with the Heavenly Stem and forming a Punishment 刑 with the Earthly Branch this configuration foretells complex emotions. The presence of the Heaven Stem is an indication of a positive exterior but the Punishment indicates that behind this disguise the individual may actually be quite unhappy.

This configuration may appear in the BaZi Natal Chart in the Year, Month or Hour Pillars. It may also be found in the Luck Pillars and the Annual Pillar.

When it is located in the Year Pillar of the Natal Chart, this configuration indicates that the individual will appear, at least superficially, to have a good relationship with their grandparents but the reality will be a rather tense and emotionally distant affair.

When this configuration is found in the Month Pillar, the individual will go through the motions of a relationship with their parents but they may lack for any profound connection. This detachment may well stem from tensions and disagreements that have never been fully addressed or rectified.

A position in the Month Pillar may also be an indication of underlying discord in the work place. On the surface their relationships with their colleagues and supervisor may appear to be quite positive but the politics behind closed doors may leave the individual feeling quite stressed. It is likely however that these problems are stemming from their own attitudes and behaviours, and that they will need to work through their own emotions before they will be able to find any kind of resolution.

The presence of this configuration in the Hour Pillar is an indication that the individual may be inclined to over promise and under deliver. They need to learn to understand that it will cause less conflict in the long run if they simply decline a task that they cannot complete.

Located in the Luck Pillar, this configuration suggests that the individual will be plagued with self-doubt. They will be successful and admired but their lack of faith in their own abilities will leave them fearful that they do not deserve their accomplishments. They may run the risk of sabotaging their own futures if they cannot develop greater self-esteem.

When this configuration is in the Annual Pillar promising deals and arrangements may be placed on hold or abandoned altogether at the last minute. The individual is advised to be calm and remain focused. Their own fears and insecurities are likely to be the cause of all their problems.

Heaven Combine Earth Harm 天合地害
Ding Wei 丁未 (Fire Goat) + Ren Zi 壬子 (Water Rat)

Despite the presence of the Heavenly Stem, the formation of a Harm 害 in the presence of Earthly Branch indicates negative emotion. Again the individual is likely to maintain a positive facade but uncertainty, confusion and even fears over disloyalty my taint their relationships

This configuration can occur in the BaZi Natal Chart in the Year, Month or Hour Pillars as well as the Luck and Annual Pillars.

Should the arrangement be present in the Year Pillar, these hidden emotions will be at play in the individual's relationship with their grandparents. There may appear to be a loving bond here but the relationship will be marked by the effects of distrust and insecurity. This same emotion is also likely to surface in the individual's relationship with their friends and wider social circles as these are also represented by the Year Pillar.

Found in the Month Pillar, this configuration will indicate that the Ding Wei will more than likely maintain the pretense of a warm relationship with their parents while in reality they will be battling with uncertainty and fears over the stability of the connection. It may for them to try to address these issues before matters escalate. These hidden emotions may also have an impact on the workplace as the Month Pillar also represents career. The individual may battle with fears over the loyalty of their colleagues and supervisors.

In the Hour Pillar, this configuration suggests that the individual will struggle with hidden fears about their relationship with their children or about their connection with their clients and customers. These relationships may suffer from a lack of trust and security. Alternatively a position here may indicate that the individual will be unable to find direction in life, they may be unable to develop concrete plans their hopes and dreams may prove elusive.

When located in the Luck Pillar, the Heaven Combine Earth Harm may be an indication that success and achievement may fail to bring about peace of mind or any sense of accomplishment. The individual is likely to feel quite victimized by their working relationships.

Found in the Annual Pillar and this configuration implies that the individual will appear to have quite a successful year but that they will be left unsatisfied by their achievements. It is likely that jealousy is clouding their judgment and they may need to reassess their perception of what they have without comparing it and finding it wanting.

Heaven Friend Earth Clash 天比地沖
Ding Wei 丁未 (Fire Goat) + Ding Chou 丁丑 (Fire Ox)

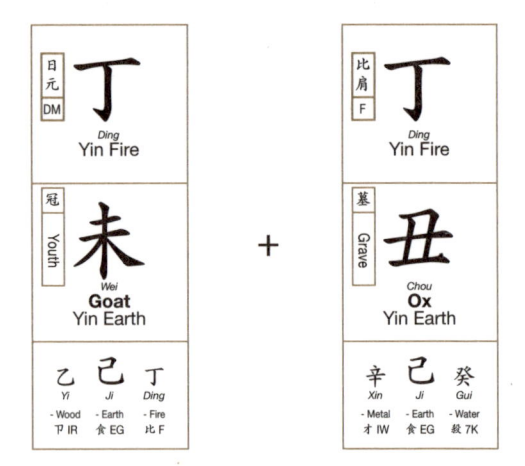

This Pillar signifies that agreements may be made only to be broken. Promises may fail to live up to expectation. It is likely that plans will go astray and events may not unfold as anticipated. The individual is likely to feel disappointed but they need to remember that the unexpected is not always a bad thing. In this case the Heavenly Stem will dictate whether the ultimate outcome is a positive or a negative. If the Heavenly Stem is favorable it will all turn out to be for the best.

This combination can be found in the BaZi Natal Chart in the Year, Month or Hour Pillars. It can also appear in the Luck Pillars and the Annual Pillar.

In the Year, Month or Hour Pillars, these emotions and events are likely to play out in connection to and with impact upon the individual's relationships. In the Year Pillar, it will be their relationship with their grandparents or their friends that comes under strain.

In the Month Pillar, it will be the relationship with their parents that will be affected. As the Moth Pillar also represents the individual's professional life it is possible they will also find that their relationships with their colleagues, or even their career in general, is effected by unexpected twists and turns.

In the Hour Pillar, it will be their relationship with their children, their clients or their employees that may be unsettled. A position in the Hour Pillar can also show its effects in the feeling the individual has about their contribution to the world and also to their hopes, dreams and aspirations. A good idea may fail to come to fruition or an unexpected event may change their perspectives. It is possible that they will find they are unable to reach their goals or they may change their mind about what they had hoped for in life and dramatically changed direction.

A period of steady and gradual change is likely should this configuration be apparent in the Luck Pillar. This may be a painful time but it will also be a time of learning. The valuable lessons that the individual is able to take away with them will make the outcome a positive.

When the Heaven Friend Earth Clash is found in the Annual Pillar, the individual will fight many private battles in a year of tumultuous twists and turns. They will learn a great deal about themselves during this time and will emerge enriched by the experience.

Heaven and Earth Clash 天冲地冲
Ding Wei 丁未 (Fire Goat) + Gui Chou 癸丑 (Water Ox)

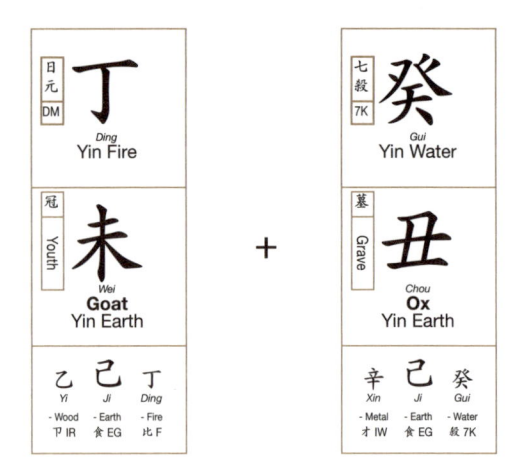

丁 Ding — Yin Fire (日元 DM)
未 Wei Goat — Yin Earth (冠 Youth)
  乙 Yi - Wood 卩 IR
  己 Ji - Earth 食 EG
  丁 Ding - Fire 比 F

+

癸 Gui — Yin Water (七殺 7K)
丑 Chou Ox — Yin Earth (墓 Grave)
  辛 Xin - Metal 才 IW
  己 Ji - Earth 食 EG
  癸 Gui - Water 殺 7K

This configuration is also called the unlucky formation or Fan Yin 反吟 formation. It clashes inward toward the Ding Wei and has the effect of draining the good qualities of their Day Pillar. In addition to making it harder for the Ding Wei individual to achieve success on their own merits, it may also act to put further obstacles in their way.

This configuration may also impact upon the Ding Wei if it appears in the Chart of someone they know. As individual who has this configuration in their chart may have a negative influence on the Ding Wei's life. Though they may be good people with good intentions they may also be the source of poor advice.

The Heaven Counter Earth Clash configuration may appear in this BaZi Natal Chart in the Year, Month or Hour Pillars. It may also be found in the Luck and the Annual Pillars.

If the combination is in the Year Pillar, the individual is likely to have a poor connection with their grandparents. The Year Pillar also indicates friends and social networking and it possible that the individual will struggle to make the right connections and this may impair their chances of personal and professional success.

When the placement of this configuration is in the Month Pillar, the individual's relationship with their parents or may be negatively influenced. The Month Pillar also represents their career and it is equally possible that they will struggle to find the right job or they may be unable to make much professional progress.

When seen in the Hour Pillar, this combination represents an inability to form a positive connection with their children and with their employees. It could be that they have to juggle too many tasks to be able to have the time to really develop these relationships. The Hour Pillar also governs a person's dreams and ambitions in life and it could be that the individual find it hard to achieve their goals.

Should this configuration be located in the Luck Pillar, the individual is likely to be confronted with a series of obstacles and challenges throughout a ten-year luck cycle. They are advised to remain calm and optimistic as these experiences will help to make them stronger and they will be better equipped to face any problems that the future may bring.

If the Heaven and Earth Clash appears in the Annual Pillar, the individual would be wise to try to live quietly and keep a low profile for the year. They should not make any major changes, if at all possible, and they should avoid becoming involved in any new investments.

Heaven Counter Earth Clash 天剋地沖
Ding Wei 丁未 (Fire Goat) + Xin Chou 辛丑 (Metal Ox)

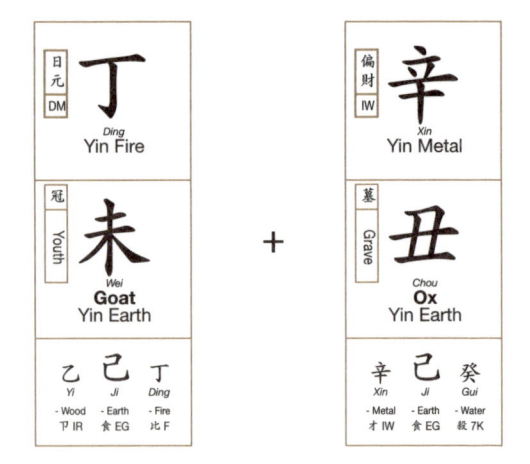

日元 DM	丁 Ding Yin Fire		偏財 IW	辛 Xin Yin Metal
冠 Youth	未 Wei Goat Yin Earth	+	墓 Grave	丑 Chou Ox Yin Earth
乙 Yi -Wood 卩 IR	己 Ji -Earth 食 EG	丁 Ding -Fire 比 F	辛 Xin -Metal 才 IW	己 Ji -Earth 食 EG	癸 Gui -Water 殺 7K

The Heaven Counter Earth Clash Pillar is a formation in which the Day Pillar forms a clash with the Xin Chou 辛丑. It is important to note that this configuration and the Heaven and Earth Clash formation are different. This situation places the individual in a position of control. As such, these individuals are likely to be endowed with a strong desire for victory and for achieving success in life. Good entrepreneur skills are also often indicated by this formation.

This arrangement can be found in the BaZi Natal Chart, in the Year, Month and Hour Pillars as well as in the Luck and Annual Pillars.

If this configuration is placed in the Year Pillar the individual is likely to receive help in the form of the support and advice of high-profile friends. The individual is, however, advised not to rely solely on this help and assistance if they want to achieve their dreams. Their own hard work will be integral if they are to capitalize on the head start their friends are able to give them.

In the Month Pillar, this configuration suggests an individual with a keen business sense. They will have what it takes to build and run a business and they will be capable of turning a tidy profit. However, they will need avoid being too greedy and allowing avarice to cloud their judgment.

An individual who considers their career to be their utmost priority is indicated by the placement of this formation in the Hour Pillar. These individuals will struggle to find time for personal relationships and they be need to be reminded that happiness cannot be based on professional success alone.

The individual will uncover a series of financial opportunities that will bring them material wealth when this configuration is found in the Luck Pillar. Again, they mustn't be swayed by their drive for profits and greed and they should be careful to think clearly about their actions.

This configuration is an indication of one that will find success in new partnerships and business ventures, when this formation is found in the Annual Pillar. Their personal life will be compensated in their quest for a better and more promising professional life.

丁未

Fire Goat

Heaven and Earth Unity 天同地比
Ding Wei 丁未 (Fire Goat) + Ding Wei 丁未 (Wood Goat)

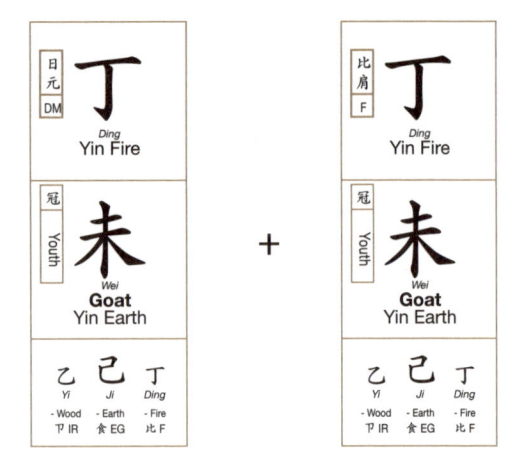

Traditionally referred to as the Fu Yin 伏吟 formation, this configuration is an indication of sadness, distress and emotional pain. It is also often called the Hidden Warning Pillar.

It can be found in the BaZi Natal Chart in the Year, Month and Hour Pillars and in the Luck and Annual Pillars.

When found in the Year Pillar, it may suggest that the individual has quite a poor relationship with their grandparents. It is even possible that they may never have had the opportunity to meet their grandparents. The Year Pillar also had an influence over the individual's friends and networking, and a placement here could indicate that the individual may not always be able to spare the time to be with their friends or to develop a social life.

When located in the Month Pillar, this configuration is thought to be an indication that the relationship the individual shares with their parents may be strained. They may struggle to be abler to connect to their parents in any meaningful way. This may also be an indication that the parents are unable or unwilling to leave an inheritance or to involve the individual in the family business. These same feelings have the potential also to surface in the workplace, where the individual's relationships with colleagues and superiors may come under strain.

In the Hour Pillar, this configuration can imply that the individual is not as close to their children as might be desired. They may find that they are unable to spend a lot of time with their children and this may mean that they struggle to be able to relate to them or develop as meaningful a relationship as they would hope for. In more extreme cases it could be that they have been separated from their children or they may be unable to have a family. A position here may also connect to the individuals dreams and goals and it could be that they will find that they are struggling to achieve all that they had hoped.

This configuration in the Luck Pillar indicates a spiritual path. The individual may take up a religious vocation or religion and spirituality could simply be an important part of their lives. Alternatively they may be very focused on their health. Sadly this can also indicate the loss of a parent.

When this arrangement appears in the Annual Pillar, the individual is likely to have a very successful year in terms of career and material gains but there is likely to be a distressing emotional even that casts a shadow over the year.

Heaven and Earth Combo 天地相合
Ding Wei 丁未 (Fire Goat) + Ren Wu 壬午 (Water Horse)

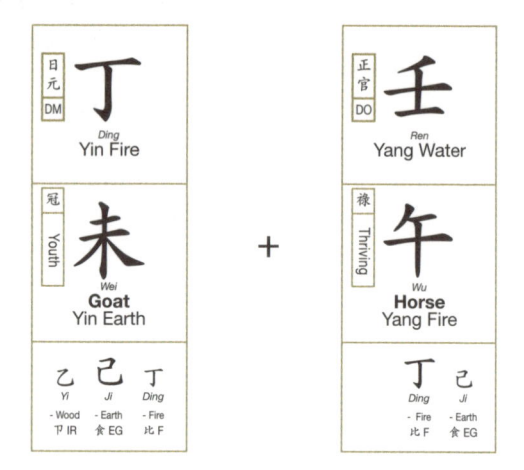

日元 DM	丁 Ding Yin Fire		正官 DO	壬 Ren Yang Water
冠 Youth	未 Wei Goat Yin Earth	+	祿 Thriving	午 Wu Horse Yang Fire
乙 Yi - Wood 卩 IR	己 Ji - Earth 食 EG	丁 Ding - Fire 比 F	丁 Ding - Fire 比 F	己 Ji - Earth 食 EG

This is the most desirable Pillar of all. It symbolizes good relationships that bring with them success and happiness.

When this configuration is present in the Chart of one connected to the Ding Wei, it is an indication, not only that this person will enjoy a particular affinity with the Ding Wei individual, but that they are also likely to be of help in a time of need.

This configuration can be found in the Year, Month or Hour Pillars as well as the Luck Pillar and the Annual Pillars.

If found in the Year Pillar, the Heaven and Earth Combine configuration indicates that the individual will be quite close their grandparents and they are likely to enjoy spending many happy times together. It is also likely that they will have loyal friends and good social status.

When this configuration is found in the Month Pillar, the individual is likely to have a strong bond with their parents. There is also a good indication that they will have the appreciation of their superiors at work, which may increase their chances of career progression in the future.

If this arrangement is found in the Hour Pillar, it is an indication that the individual is likely to have a warm and loving relationship with their children. They are also likely to be able to rely upon the support and respect of their employees, clients and suppliers.

Should this arrangement be found in either the Luck or the Annual Pillar, the individual will be happy in all their personal, familial and romantic relationships. They are also likely to see career success through partnerships and joint ventures.

Rob Wealth Goat Blade 劫財羊刃
Ding Wei 丁未 (Fire Goat) + Bing Wu 丙午 (Fire Horse)

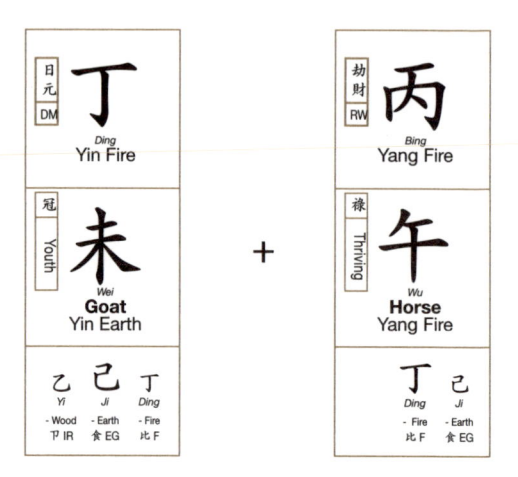

日元 DM	丁 Ding Yin Fire		劫財 RW	丙 Bing Yang Fire
冠 Youth	未 Wei Goat Yin Earth	+	祿 Thriving	午 Wu Horse Yang Fire

Ding Wei hidden stems: 乙 Yi - Wood 才 IR, 己 Ji - Earth 食 EG, 丁 Ding - Fire 比 F

Bing Wu hidden stems: 丁 Ding - Fire 比 F, 己 Ji - Earth 食 EG

The Rob Wealth Goat Blade 劫財羊刃 configuration indicates potential financial losses regardless of where it appears in the individual's Chart. It could bring forth issues relating to financial management, a downtime in your investment or a period of high expenditure.

Should this configuration appear in the Chart of someone connected to the Ding Wei, this person is likely to be the cause of the Ding Wei losing money. This may not be due to any intent on their part, it may be something as simple as the Bing Wu being inclined to overspend when they are together.

丁酉

Ding You

丁丑 Ding Chou 丁卯 Ding Mao 丁巳 Ding Si 丁未 Ding Wei 丁酉 Ding You 丁亥 Ding Hai

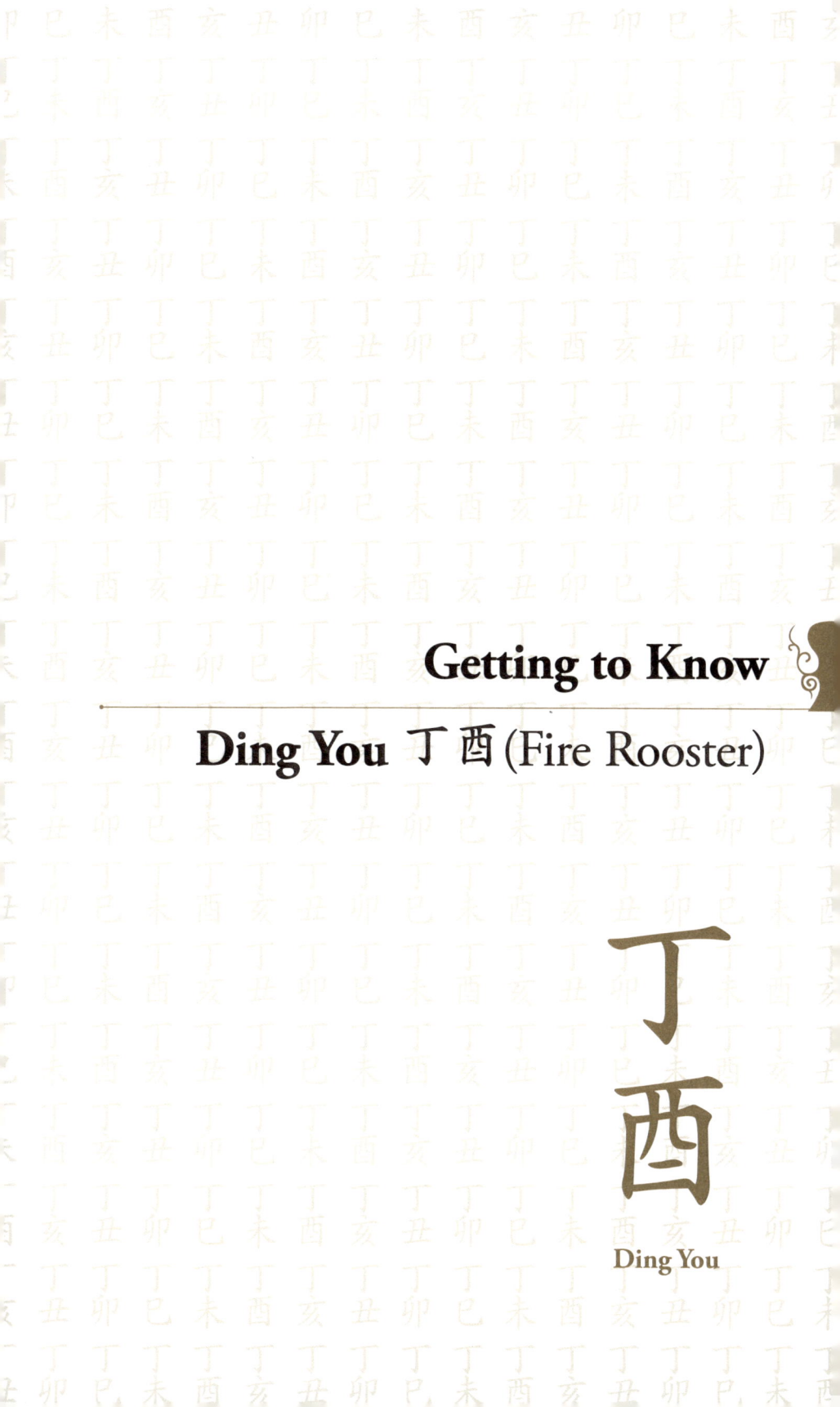

Getting to Know
Ding You 丁酉 (Fire Rooster)

丁酉

Ding You

Positive Imagery

丁酉 Fire Rooster

Negative Imagery

八字一柱論命法

丁酉

Fire Rooster

Getting to Know
Ding You 丁酉 (Fire Rooster)

General Observations:

The image that represents the Ding You is one in which light is reflected on polished surfaces and veneers. It is no wonder then that the words like positive, exuberant, attractive, eye-catching and talented best describe Ding You individuals.

As their imagery suggests Ding You individuals revel in the limelight; they love to take center stage and be noticed for their talents and they almost always are. The Ding You are incredibly charismatic individuals who exude confidence and charm and have the power to draw people to them. Social and active, Ding You individuals make friends easily and they enjoy meeting new people and developing new connections. They thrive in the company of like-minded and intelligent individuals from whom they can learn new perspectives and through whom they are able to expand and develop their circles and open new doors.

Ding You individuals are highly ambitious and determined. Once they have committed to a goal or project, they will work with tireless perseverance to get the job done. Optimistic and innovative with a can do attitude, far from being defeated by a challenge or a setback, the Ding You will, instead, regard it as an opportunity to improve their skills and demonstrate their abilities. They have no fear of developing dynamic new approaches in order to overcome any obstacle placed in their path and they will happily abandon unsuccessful strategies in favour of new tactics in order to push forward with their endeavours.

Open minded, inventive and creative, the Ding You is often able to link ideas and concepts together to create exciting new insights and breakthroughs. Such abilities are often thought to be the very building blocks of genius and the Ding You often excels where they are given the freedom to pursue their instincts and observations without interference. They are very independent spirits who will buck at restriction and overly dominant authority.

The Ding You are often far more comfortable with a position of command than they are with one of deference. They are action oriented and self-motivated, which when combined with their excellent people skills often makes them exceptionally gifted leaders. Persuasive and passionate, they can be truly inspirational and they seldom lack for supporters for their ventures. Though they can be impatient and short tempered, they are also motivational and they will quickly overcome their short bursts of temper in order to find a practical resolution to their dilemmas.

Ding You individuals are naturally drawn toward a rather glamorous lifestyle. They have a great appreciation of style and beauty and they will surround themselves will items that reflect this and which inspire them to keep achieving. Though they may be sophisticated in their tastes however they are straightforward in their emotions. Decisive and forthright, they are very clear about their needs and desires in a relationship and will be fully committed once their hearts have been engaged. These special individuals will equally act to support and inspire them throughout their lives and will give them a firm foundation from which to grow and demonstrate their extraordinary potential.

Key Character Traits of the Ding You 丁酉: Overall

- Creative
- Practical
- Compassionate
- Hardworking
- Strong-willed
- Enthusiastic

Work Life

丁酉

Ding You

Professional Self

The Ding You's natural commanding presence helps them to succeed in their career life. They have good imagination, which helps them to produce exceptional results at work especially in the creative fields.

The Ding You are confident and are usually capable of embracing the leadership role. They can unite everyone towards a common goal. As a leader, they are also sensitive to their followers' needs and feelings.

Good practical, organizational skills are also their strong points. They bring efficient management to their work, and would make a great asset to any company. In addition, they are more proactive about expanding their knowledge and skills for professional and personal development.

Career Options

The Ding You individuals are principle-centered. They are the ones who will fight for a cause they strongly believe in. The Ding You also have a flair for words and making connections. These traits will serve them well if they pursue a political career. They make good statesmen, and these roles will help them become the catalyst for better change in the country.

They have a talent for the written word and visual media. As such, they are able to make a career as a writer, or in the photography or film industry. The Ding You are also creative, and will find a calling in the fields of advertising, public relations and design. They would also make charismatic teachers and trainers, and their persuasive nature would help them do well in sales or promotion.

Key Character Traits of the Ding You 丁酉: Work life

Positive

- Independent
- Good organizer
- Dedicated
- Enthusiastic
- Hardworking

Negative

- Stubborn
- Careless
- Overbearing
- Judgmental
- Overly critical

Love and Relationships

丁酉

Ding You

Love

Ding You individuals are honest, sympathetic, loyal and compassionate when it comes to love. They are most expressive when they are with a partner who shares their ideas. The Ding You may jump from one relationship to another, in order to search for a partner that fulfils their definition of The One in life. Because of this, they need to remain as patient when it comes to matters of love and relationship.

Once they find the perfect person, Ding You individuals are likely to be unwaveringly devoted to their partner or spouse. They view this commitment as their responsibility to uphold the positive connection in the relationship.

Acquaintances

All the Ding You have to do is be themselves, as they are naturally charming, and others will flock to them. They are sociable and will very often find themselves most interested in acquaintances who are creative and hardworking. These are the types of individuals that stimulate the same qualities in Ding You individuals.

Ding You individuals enjoy an active exchange of ideas that stimulate their creativity. Because of this, they tend to seek acquaintances in people with liked-minded view and as such, majority of their friends are derived from their workplace or common-interest group.

They may be difficult to analyze at times because what they project on the surface many not exactly portray how they truly feel. Only a handful of trusted confidantes in their circle would see their hidden personality.

Family

The Ding You is generous, affectionate and caring when they are with those that they love. They receive their hope and inspiration from personal relationships, which means a loving atmosphere, is vital for them.

Ding You individuals are likely to be loyal throughout the years of their marriage, regardless of the circumstances. They take the adage "for better and for worse" seriously.

They make certain to keep peace and harmony in the household and maintain this atmosphere by talking the issues over with the other members of the household. A good communication in a spousal relation can ensure things are progressing positively for them.

They should make certain to guard themselves from mood swings and impulsive action.

Key Character Traits of the Ding You 丁酉: Love & Relationships

- Sympathetic
- Devoted
- Loving
- Loyal
- Protective
- Charming

Famous Personalities

Alexander Graham Bell - Scottish scientist, inventor, engineer and innovator. He is known for his invention of the telephone.

Camilla Parker - Duchess of Cornwall, and the second wife of Charles, Prince of Wales.

Usain Bolt – Jamaican sprinter, who is widely regarded as the fastest person ever. He is the first man to win six Olympic gold medals in sprinting, and an eight-time World champion.

Source: Wikipedia *(June 2013)*

Technical Analysis

丁酉

Ding You

BaZi Day Pillar Analytics 日柱分析

時 Hour	日 Day	月 Month	年 Year	
	日元 DM 丁 Ding Yin Fire			天干 Heavenly Stems
	生 Growth 酉 You Rooster Yin Metal			地支 Earthly Branches
	辛 Xin - Metal 才 IW			藏干 Hidden Stems

丁酉 — Fire Rooster

The Ding You 丁酉 Pillar sits on the Growth 長生 position in the 12 Growth Phases theory of BaZi as well as the Indirect Wealth Star 偏財星. This Pillar is also considered to be supported by the Night Noble and the Intelligence Star, which indicates that Ding You individuals are Noble (in this application of the word 'noble' indicates that they are helpful and may act as mentors to those around them), intelligent, knowledgeable and well-respected. Because Yin Fire and Yin Metal are two opposites, this configuration also denotes that the Ding You individual has the potential to have a somewhat rebellious nature.

Ding You individuals are capable of displaying great strength, creativity and power. They are inventive and extremely intelligent and can demonstrate tremendous feats of concentration and endurance. Therefore, the Ding You is sometimes imagined as being like the strong beam of a laser, blasted onto a metal surface. True to this image, they are seen to possess focus, consistency and energy in their work, just as the beam that slowly carves, creates and sculpts the metal block.

The Ding You will often like to be in control, taking responsibility for their own actions. This is the nature indicated by the Yin Metal Indirect Wealth Star. Preferring to make their own choices, they will never rush to a decision, instead cautious and analytical, they will think through all of the facts and figures. As they are perfectionist by nature, they can sometimes lack faith in themselves especially when they are overwhelmed by problems and this can result in uncertainty and inertia. Despite this they will be very reluctant to accept advice and they may need to learn to recognize genuine help when it is offered rather than groundless criticism or interference. This is represented by the You 酉 (Rooster) making a hidden-pull to the Chen 辰 (Dragon) or the Hurting Officer Star 傷官星.

Despite all of their drive, the Ding You can also be fickle and they are frequently restless. They are idealists, constantly searching for inner peace and they are frequently dissatisfied. Always chasing after new experiences and new ventures, they may have a tendency to spread themselves too thin across too many projects. They are, however, enthusiastic and courageous, very direct, ambitious and enterprising.

The Ding You individual tends to be rather reserved. They can be emotionally intense and they often struggle to be able to express their feelings or opinions. This is because the You 酉 (Rooster) makes a hidden-clash with the Mao 卯 (Rabbit), the Ding's Resource element. They are however very shrewd and intuitive judges of character and they may know and understand the thoughts and motives of others without needing to ask. They have a fierce sense of independence and they may, at times, appear to be a law unto themselves. Behind all this however they have a yearning to be part of a group and they are capable of being extremely loving and generous.

The Ding You has a real love of home and family and they often make exceptional parents. They will happily extend their strength into the care and support of their loved ones but they need to guard against becoming too controlling. They can be impatient and intolerant but they are also often able to inspire people with their powerful demeanor and they will always be able to find support for their causes.

Technical Observations

The Ding You 丁酉 Pillar favors a meeting with a Ren 壬 and Yi 乙 in the Chart. These Stems, represent the Direct Officer Star 正官星 and Indirect Resource Star 偏印星 and they bring the necessary balance and stability to the Ding You individual. Take note, however, that even though both of these elements are Water and Wood, it would be unfavourable for this Pillar to meet with Gui 癸 and Jia 甲 Stems instead. This is because Gui 癸 is the 7 Killings Star 七殺星 which directly puts out the already weak Ding Fire and Jia Wood is the Direct Resource 正印 which the frail Ding Fire will find hard to consume as the wood is too strong and sturdy.

八字一柱論命法

丁酉
Fire Rooster

Punishment, Clash or Destruction formations by the Xu 戌 (Dog) and the Mao 卯 (Rabbit) with this Pillar are also highly unfavourable, as these would further destabilize the already fragile Yin Fire. If these configurations are present the individual is likely to struggle to achieve in life and they will face a great many challenges and obstacles.

The You 酉 (Rooster) is the Nobleman Star 貴人星 of the Ding Fire. In this context, since the Rooster is of the Metal element, it relates to monetary concerns. This suggests that the Ding You will have helpful people in their life who will support them with regard to finance. That is why, in most cases, Ding You individuals are usually able to become quite wealthy. However, should a clash, combination, harm or punishment be present in the Branches of the Chart or in the Luck Pillars, this auspicious attribute would be negated.

If the Resource Star 印星 is in the Chart of a male Ding You, it denotes that his wife may clash with his mother. They are likely to struggle to see eye to eye and the conflict may be profound enough to mean that they would not be able to cohabit in the same home. This is especially true should his wife be a Xin 辛 Metal Day Master. Interestingly, she will not only employ methods to get rid of her mother-in-law, but she will also make it appear as if it were her husband's choice. Another point of interest is that most Ding You men tend to prefer a much younger wife.

The female Ding You tends to be beautiful and elegant. Both the Ding 丁 and You 酉 are part of the Trigram Dui 兌 (in the Ba Gua), which represents a young, pretty woman. These women are usually exceptionally physically attractive.

Those born in the Spring and Summer months tend to be less emotional by nature. Those born in the Winter and Autumn months tend to be little more prudent and diligent and as a result are often very successful. Born during the day time (5AM – 5PM), Ding You individuals will have to work hard because the flame of the candle of the Ding is less bright during these times, they are unlikely to benefit from a great deal of support and they will have to rely upon their own efforts to achieve success. Those who are born at night (5PM – 5AM) are far more likely to be find happiness and fulfillment. This is because the Ding Fire, being the candle fire, shines much brighter during these hours. It is undesirable for the Ding You to be born in the Xu 戌 (Dog) month, as these individuals are likely to face a life of toil and challenges, they will struggle to achieve their goals as there will be a great many obstacles placed in their path.

Unique 60 Pillar Combinations

This section covers the relationships between the individual pillar under this elemental polarity and several other pillars found in the 60 Jia Zi cycle.

丁
酉

Ding You

Heaven Combine Earth Harm 天合地害
Ding You 丁酉 (Fire Rooster) + Ren Xu 壬戌 (Water Dog)

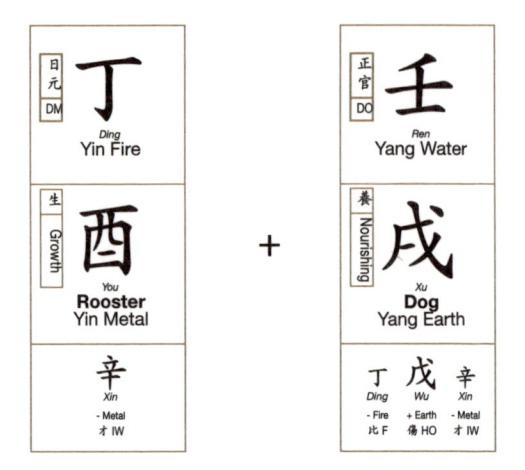

日元 DM	正官 DO
丁 Ding — Yin Fire	壬 Ren — Yang Water
生 Growth	養 Nourishing
酉 You — Rooster — Yin Metal	戌 Xu — Dog — Yang Earth
辛 Xin — Metal — 才 IW	丁 Ding - Fire 比 F / 戊 Wu + Earth 傷 HO / 辛 Xin - Metal 才 IW

In this configuration, although the Heavenly Stem is present a Harm 害 is formed with the Earthly Branch. The result of this is that the individual is likely to appear to be very happy and successful but they will be hiding feelings of confusion and unhappiness stemming from issues of loyalty.

Should this configuration occur in the Year Pillar, those hidden emotions will be connected to the individual's grandparents. The relationship will appear warm and congenial on the surface but the Ding You is likely to feel unsure and even distrustful. The Year Pillar also signifies social connections and friendship circles. With a placement here the individual may find that they have mainly fair weather friends who would not be prepared to support them in a crisis.

Found in the Month Pillar, this configuration suggests that tension and uncertainty will be hidden behind the façade of a positive relationship with the individual's parents. If this individual does not work to resolve these issues there is a possibility that the relationship will deteriorate further as the years pass by. Additionally, as the Month Pillar also reflects upon the individual's professional life, it could be that the individual will have uncomfortable and uncertain relationships with their colleagues and supervisors.

If this configuration is found in the Hour Pillar, the individual is likely to be insecure about their relationship with their children or with their employees and clients despite all outward appearances to the contrary. It is important to note that the Hour Pillar can also have an impact upon the individual's hopes, dreams and aspirations. It is possible the Ding You will feel unsure of the way ahead.

When located in the Luck Pillar, the Heaven Combine Earth Harm indicates that the individual will achieve a great deal but they will believe that their success has come at a price. They are likely to feel jaded, even victimized, and they will not find any sense of satisfaction in their accomplishments.

If found in the Annual Pillar, this configuration suggests that what should have been a good year will conclude in dissatisfaction and frustration. The individual will be disappointed by their accomplishments but they need to be aware that their judgment may well be impaired by jealousy.

Heaven Friend Earth Clash 天比地冲
Ding You 丁酉 (Fire Rooster) + Ding Mao 丁卯 (Fire Rabbit)

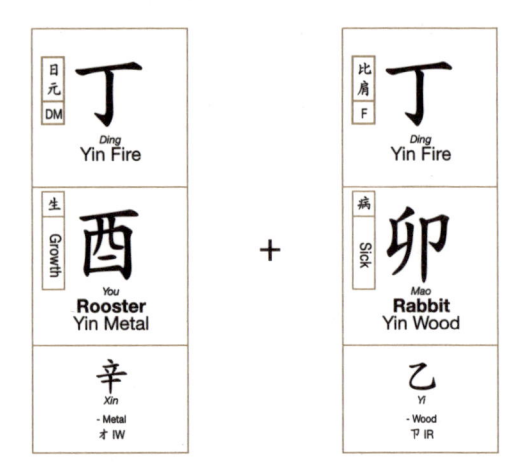

日元 DM	丁 Ding Yin Fire		比肩 F	丁 Ding Yin Fire
生 Growth	酉 You Rooster Yin Metal	+	病 Sick	卯 Mao Rabbit Yin Wood
	辛 Xin - Metal 才 IW			乙 Yi - Wood 卩 IR

This configuration suggests that agreements may initially be reached but that they will fall apart due to a change in circumstances. Promises may fail to live up to expectation and plans may go astray. The individual is likely to feel frustrated and disillusioned but it would serve them well to remember that the unexpected is not always bad. An unanticipated turn of events may yet turn out to have positive ramifications. This will all depend on the nature of the Heavenly Stem. Individuals with this formation in their chart are also likely to be very active but achieve little of note. They may be making empty efforts.

This configuration can be found in the BaZi Natal Chart in the Year, Month or Hour Pillars. It can also appear in the Luck Pillars and the Annual Pillar.

When this configuration appears in the Year, Month or Hour Pillars it is likely to have an impact on the individual's relationships.

Unforeseen circumstances could be source of tension in their relationship with their grandparents if found the Year Pillar. Equally a position here indicates that these feelings may extend beyond the individual's familial relationships and it could be that the individual is unsettled in their wider social circles too. It could be that their relationships with their friends are tumultuous and unpredictable.

If found in the Month Pillar, this configuration suggests that, tension is likely to surface in the individual's relationship with their parents. Quarrels may result from an unexpected turn of events and the individual may find that this is exacerbated by a lack of communication. Career and professional relationships are also governed by the Month Pillar and the individual may find that their connections with their managers and colleagues are effected by a change in their working conditions.

The connection with their children, clients or suppliers may be unexpectedly destabilized if this configuration is seen in the Hour Pillar. The Hour Pillar also has a connection to the individuals, hopes and aspirations and a position here can also be an indication that a great concept may fall apart in the application or that the individual's opinion of their contribution to the world is dramatically altered. In this case the individual is advised not to lose hope too easily, they should take time to relook or reflect on the situation before moving forward again. Remember that the impact of the Heavenly Stem could mean that there are fortuitous outcomes to be gained from apparently negative turns of event.

When this configuration surfaces in the Luck Pillar, the individual will go through a period of slow and painful change. This will be a difficult time but the lessons learned and ultimate outcome will both prove to have a positive impact.

The Heaven Friend Earth Clash found in the Annual Pillar indicates that the year will be fraught with unexpected twists and turns. The individual is likely to have to fight some private battles but they will be rewarded with self-discovery and rich personal experience.

Heaven Friend Earth Punish 天比地刑
Ding You 丁酉 (Fire Rooster) + Ding You 丁酉 (Wood Rooster)

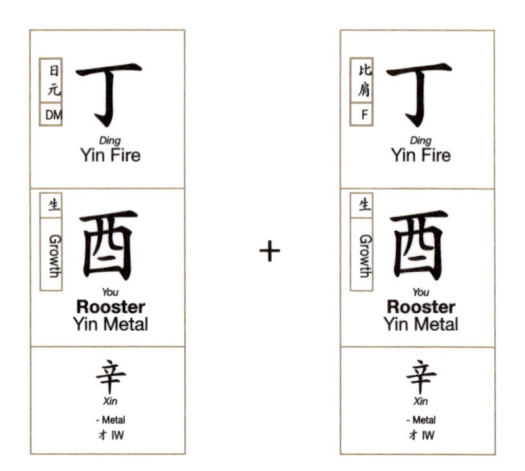

日元 DM	丁 Ding Yin Fire		比肩 F	丁 Ding Yin Fire
Growth	酉 You **Rooster** Yin Metal 辛 Xin - Metal 才 IW	+	Growth	酉 You **Rooster** Yin Metal 辛 Xin - Metal 才 IW

This Heaven Friend Earth Punish should not be confused with the Heavenly Combine and Earthly Punish even though they may appear to be similar. In this setting no configuration is formed instead the appearance of the Friend Star 比肩星 in the Stem signifies that the Self is the theme of the Pillar. The individual will have to battle with their own emotions in a journey of self-discovery during which they may experience some pain and distress.

The Heaven Friend Earth Punish may be found in the BaZi Natal Chart in the Year, Month, or Hour Pillars as well as the Luck and Annual Pillars.

When located in the Year Pillar, this configuration suggests that the Ding You will feel rather anxious and insecure about their relationship with their grandparents. They may fear that they cannot live up to their grandparents' expectations. A placement here could also suggest problems stemming from the individual's connections with their friends and wider acquaintance as the Year Pillar also indicates social circles and networking. It is possible that the individual will feel quite shy and socially awkward.

In the Month Pillar, this configuration will, instead, have an impact upon the individual's relationship with their parents. They may feel that they are incapable of fulfilling their parents' hopes and dreams for them. Their parents may not share their fears, however, and much of their insecurity could be coming from their own lack of confidence.

This formation may also have an effect on the individual's career. They may be consumed by work related stress. It is possible that they will feel overwhelmed by their job role and they may struggle to connect with their colleagues. Alternatively they may find that they are carrying the workload of a mismatched and underperforming team. Equally it may be that many of their problems are imagined and they may need to work on their confidence and open themselves up to trusting and fulfilling working relationships.

When this configuration is found in the Hour Pillar it is possible that the individual may worry that they are failing as a parent. They may be concerned that are not able to adequately provide for their children or that they are not offering them enough emotional support. They will feel this way even if their children are happy and healthy. The Hour Pillar can also act to influence how the individual feels about their path in life and on their long terms hopes, goals and aspirations. It is possible that these individuals will be reluctant to try to pursue their dreams for fear of failure.

Should this configuration appear in the Luck Pillar, the individual will face a series of challenges and obstacles, their pride or confidence may be bruised but this will be a period of learning and growth and the ending may prove to be bittersweet. The individual is advised to be patient and focused and maintain faith in their loved ones.

When the Heaven Friend Earth Punish is located in the Annual Pillar, the individual is likely to be attracted to a series of new relationships, connections and flirtations. There is potential for fun to be had but the individual may find that they are distracted from their careers and it may be wise for them to try to remain focused.

Heaven and Earth Clash 天沖地沖
Ding You 丁酉 (Fire Rooster) + Gui Mao 癸卯 (Water Rabbit)

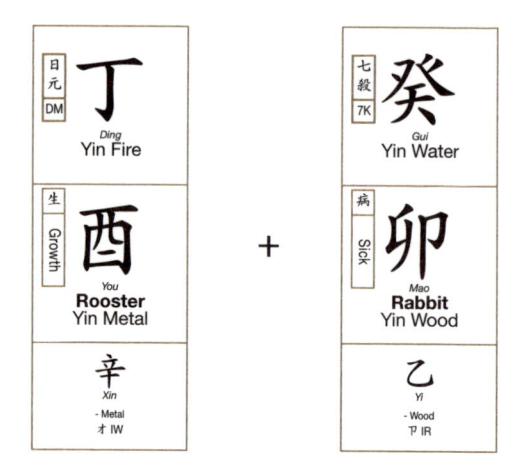

日元 DM	丁 Ding Yin Fire		七殺 7K	癸 Gui Yin Water
生 Growth	酉 You Rooster Yin Metal	+	病 Sick	卯 Mao Rabbit Yin Wood
	辛 Xin - Metal 才 IW			乙 Yi - Wood 卩 IR

This Pillar clashes inward toward the Ding You's Day Pillar and acts to drain them of their good qualities. Also known as the Fan Yin 反吟 formation, this configuration greatly impairs the individual's chances of success.

The configuration may also have an impact if it appears in the charts of people connected to the Ding You, though they may have only good intentions these individuals may very well have an unwitting negative influence.

The Heaven and Earth Clash can be found in the BaZi Natal Chart in the Year, Month and Hour Pillars as well as the Luck and Annual Pillars.

If this configuration is found in the Year Pillar, the individual is likely to have only a distant relationship with their grandparents. As the Year Pillar also impacts upon social circles and networking, it is possible that they will struggle to make friends or to make the right connections and they may have a tendency to fall into the wrong crowd.

Found in the Month Pillar, this configuration may mean that the individual will find that they are unable to form a really positive connection with their parents. Equally the Month Pillar can also influence career and it is possible that the individual will find it difficult to settle in their career path. They may also struggle to really bond with their co-workers and they may find their office environment quite challenging.

Should this configuration be placed in the Hour Pillar, the Ding You may not be as close to their children as they would like. They may have been separated from their children somehow or they may simply find it hard to form a good relationship with them. Equally it could be that these individuals will feel a little lost in the work as the Hour Pillar also connects to idea, goals and aspirations. It could be that the individual has to work to really find their place and feel that they are giving something back.

The Heaven and Earth Clash formation found in the Luck Pillars indicates that the individual will have to face many challenges and obstacles during this period. This may be a turbulent and stressful time and it would be wise for them to work to remain hopeful. They should take heart that these experiences will teach them a great deal and they will serve to help make them stronger moving forward.

When this configuration appears in the Annual Pillar, the individual is advised not to make any major changes to their personal or professional life where possible, and they should equally avoid becoming involved in any new financial investments. They may not have the best of luck during the year and it would be wise to wait patiently for the time to pass.

Heaven Counter Earth Clash 天剋地沖
Ding You 丁酉 (Fire Rooster) + Xin Mao 辛卯 (Metal Rabbit)

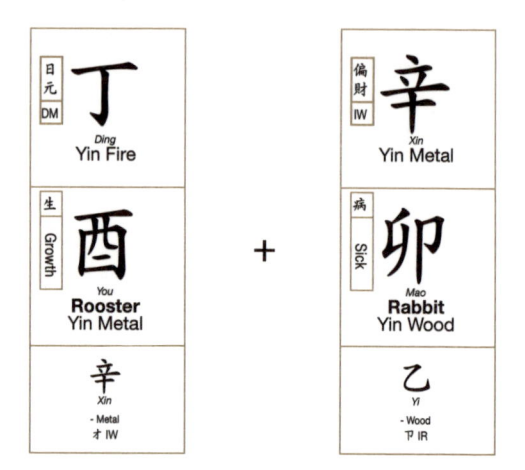

丁 Ding — Yin Fire (DM 日元)
酉 You — Rooster, Yin Metal (Growth 生) — 辛 Xin, Metal, 才 IW

+

辛 Xin — Yin Metal (IW 偏財)
卯 Mao — Rabbit, Yin Wood (Sick 病) — 乙 Yi, Wood, 卩 IR

This configuration is not to be confused with the Heaven and Earth Clash which acts to drain the individual of their positive characteristics. The Heaven Counter Earth Clash will instead act to increase their chances of success by imbibing them with a powerful need to win and to be in control. These individuals are likely to be very dominant characters and although they may at times be impatient and over hasty in the heat of their passions, their determination and entrepreneurial spirit will compel them towards greater and greater successes. This Pillar is often thought to be an indication of wealth.

This arrangement can be found in the BaZi Natal Chart, in the Year, Month and Hour Pillars as well as in the Luck and Annual Pillars.

If this configuration is placed in the Year Pillar, the individual is likely to benefit from the support and advice of wealthy and influential friends. Nevertheless they should remember that this will not be a substitute for hard work and they should not rely solely on the support they have been blessed with.

Equally they should remember to show gratitude to the Noble people that enrich their lives.

When found in the Month Pillar, this configuration suggests that the Ding You will have great business sense. They are also likely to have a talent for turning a profit. However, they may need to be wary of an inclination to become greedy or materialistic. They should always aim to treat their peers fairly and maintain a balanced view of life.

Placement in the Hour Pillar will compel the individual to focus on their career above all else. They will not find time for personal relationships. It is likely that they will need to be reminded that life about more than just work and that health and happiness depend on family and friendship.

When this configuration is found in the Luck Pillar, the individual will enjoy a series of financial opportunities that will bring them material wealth and career success. They would be advised to keep a level head during this time and to guard against greed and material desires distorting their personality.

When found in the Annual Pillar, this configuration is an indication that the individual will find success in new partnerships and business ventures. They will achieve a great deal in their professional lives but their personal lives may suffer. They are advised to make the most of the opportunities that come their way but they should also aim to make just a little time for themselves and their loved ones.

Heaven and Earth Unity 天同地比
Ding You 丁酉 (Fire Rooster) + **Ding You** 丁酉 (Wood Rooster)

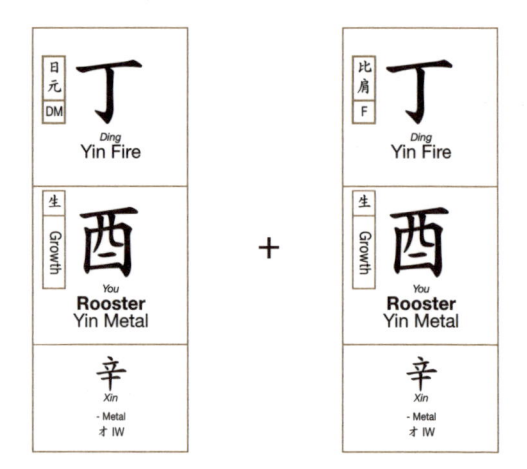

日元 DM — 丁 Ding Yin Fire	比肩 F — 丁 Ding Yin Fire
生 Growth — 酉 You Rooster Yin Metal	生 Growth — 酉 You Rooster Yin Metal
辛 Xin - Metal 才 IW	辛 Xin - Metal 才 IW

Often referred to as the Hidden Warning Pillar, the Heaven and Earth Unity is traditionally called the Fu Yin 伏吟 formation in the BaZi Chart. This configuration is an indication of sorrow and events that deal an emotional toll. In certain circumstances, this is also known as the Heaven Friend Earth Punish configuration, depending on the overall nature of the BaZi Chart.

This configuration may appear in the BaZi Natal Chart, under the Year, Month and Hour Pillars. It may also appear in the Luck and Annual Pillars.

In the Year Pillar, this configuration indicates that the individual will have a distant and unhappy relationship with their grandparents, even if they may live nearby. It is possible that they may never have even met their grandparents. The individual may also have problems connecting with their friends and developing meaningful bonds with their acquaintances.

When found in the Month Pillar, this configuration may suggest that the individual finds it very hard to connect with their parents in any meaningful way. This may be connected to or result in a loss of inheritance. The Month Pillar will also connect to the individual's career and it is possible that they may experience difficulty in establishing good working relationships with their colleagues. They may also struggle to find a profession that they truly feel passionate about.

When the Heaven and Earth Unity is found in the Hour Pillar, the individual is likely to have a weaker bond with their children than they may desire. It could be that they have been separated from their children, for instance it is possible that they may be being brought up by their grandparents. Alternatively the individual may not be able to have children.

Equally a position in the Hour Pillar could indicate that the individual will find it hard to achieve their goals. Circumstances may appear to be pushing their dreams further and further way and they may feel that they are lacking for a sense of purpose. They may indeed feel quite lost and uncertain about the future.

When this configuration is found in the Luck Pillar, it indicates an interest in spiritual matters. The individual may choose to pursue a religious vocation or religion and spirituality may simply be very important to them. Alternatively their body may become their temple and they may be very preoccupied with their health and physical well-being. Sadly a position here could also indicate the loss of a parent.

Appearing in the Annual Pillar, this configuration may point to a year of great achievements especially with regard to their careers. They are like to advance professionally and they may see an increase in their material wealth. There is a possibility however that these successes may be overshadowed by at least one distressing and emotional event.

Heaven and Earth Combo 天地相合
Ding You 丁酉 (Fire Rooster) + Ren Chen 壬辰 (Water Dragon)

日元 DM	Ding 丁 Yin Fire		正官 DO	Ren 壬 Yang Water
生 Growth	You 酉 Rooster Yin Metal	+	衰 Weakening	Chen 辰 Dragon Yang Earth
	辛 Xin − Metal 才 IW			癸 Gui − Water 殺 7K / 戊 Wu + Earth 傷 HO / 乙 Yi − Wood 卩 IR

Ding You individuals are sure to be pleased should this Pillar appear in their Chart. The Heaven and Earth Combine is the most desirable of all the formations. It is an indication that the individual will enjoy positive relationships that will impact upon their professional success and personal happiness.

The Heaven and Earth Combine is also beneficial when it is found in the Chart of someone connected to the Ding You. This individual is likely to be a good influence and they will be able to offer help and support in times of need.

When it is found in the Year Pillar, this configuration suggests that the individual is likely to have a strong connection with their grandparents. They are also likely to enjoy the company of good friends and their popularity will result in a good social status. They may also find that they are very gifted at the art of networking and they may find that they are able to open the right doors and make the right contacts.

The Month Pillar with this configuration in place suggests that the individual will have a good relationship with their parents. The Month Pillar is also likely to have an impact on the individual's ability to develop a good rapport with their colleagues and superiors and in this position is it very likely that they will enjoy a very positive working environment. This is likely to prove beneficial in terms of career progression..

Found in the Hour Pillar, this configuration is an indication that the individual is almost certain to have a warm and loving relationship with their children. They are also likely to have the respect of their employees and clients. They will have the ability to secure the trust of their customers and they will have an ability to understand their needs. As the Hour Pillar also connects to ideas and ambitions these people are also likely to be deeply connected to their goals, they will be able to develop clear plans and steer themselves towards toward making their dreams into reality.

In the Luck and Annual Pillars, the Heaven and Earth Combine configuration has the effect of enhancing relationships in all areas of the individual's individual life. Their personal relationships will be happy and fulfilling and they are likely to find career success through partnerships and joint ventures.

Rob Wealth Goat Blade 劫財羊刃
Ding You 丁酉 (Fire Rooster) + Bing Wu 丙午 (Fire Horse)

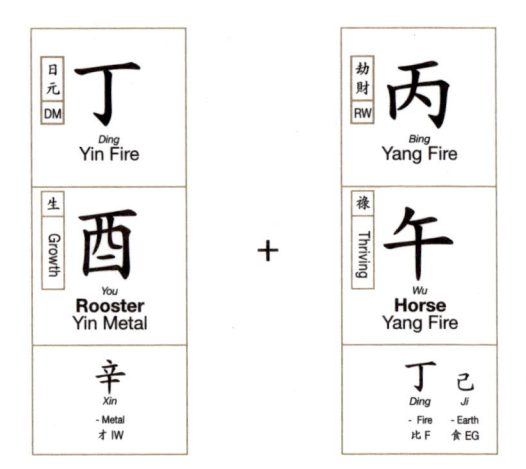

日元 DM	Ding Yin Fire	丁
生 Growth	You Rooster Yin Metal	酉
	Xin - Metal 才 IW	辛

+

劫財 RW	Bing Yang Fire	丙
祿 Thriving	Wu Horse Yang Fire	午
	Ding - Fire 比 F	Ji - Earth 食 EG	丁 己

Regardless of its position in their BaZi Chart the effect of the Rob Wealth Goat Blade 劫財羊刃 is to cause financial loss. The individual may even feel the effects of this configuration if it appears in the charts of the people around them. The presence of this configuration in another person's Chart may cause that individual to become a drain on the Ding You's resources.

The Ding You is likely to lose money just through being with them. This may not be due to any intention on their part, it may simply be that the Ding You individual tends to spend more when they are together. They may be quite happy to do so and will be unaware until much later of the cumulative effects.

丁亥

Ding Hai

丁丑 Ding Chou　丁卯 Ding Mao　丁巳 Ding Si　丁未 Ding Wei　丁酉 Ding You　丁亥 Ding Hai

Getting to Know
Ding Hai 丁亥 (Fire Pig)

丁亥

Ding Hai

Positive Imagery

Negative Imagery

八字一柱論命法

丁亥

Fire Pig

Getting to Know
Ding Hai 丁亥 (Fire Pig)

General Observations:

The Ding Hai is visually represented by the glittery light from the stars as reflected on water surfaces. Much like these glittering stars, Ding Hai individuals have an extraordinary power to mesmerize and influence others. It is quite possible that they have the potential to become an influential leader in their chosen field. History itself has revealed the brightest Ding Hai as leaders of religious or cult groups. This goes to show that if they learn to use their influence in a positive manner, they are able to affect much positive change to society.

Ding Hai individuals are independent, ambitious and idealistic. They hold natural positivism, strong endurance, and inner drive, which allow them to achieve their goals in life. These individuals are typically self-motivated with a highly creative imagination. This sense of clarity leads them to success while sheer determination and willpower leading to constant peak performance in life.

With their creative imagination, they embrace new ideas, and are often ahead of progressive trends. Driven by their own sense of idealism, they will work hard to reach their objectives. When they trust their original ideas and intuition, they can experience a straight unobstructed path to success.

Their intuition is uncannily accurate when it comes to the timing, planning and execution of projects.

When they learn to leverage on this natural intuitive power, they will discover that they "just know" when the situation is perfect. This same "voice" will also let them know when to stay away from something bad.

Since they are able to discern events swiftly, they can indeed recognize a good idea when they see one. This is why the typical Ding Hai individual can be drawn to social, political and educational reforms. These instincts can also be put to good use when meeting others for the first time as well. They will soon realize that their first impression is the most accurate.

From the career or business perspective, they have the potential to develop their own business and may use their enhanced intuitive powers to think instinctively and correctly anticipate potential business challenges and negate them before it starts. This simply means Ding Hai individuals have a natural sense of business acumen. When they reach their full potential, they can achieve their goals and create an outstanding career.

They must, however, caution from becoming overly eager or enthusiastic. Sometimes their desire to prove their productivity and success can also surface as impatience.

The Ding Hai's greatest fear is not being able to leave a legacy in life. The perfect solution would be to find a worthy cause that is both inspiring and can provide them with financial remuneration. This will help them to conquer their worrisome emotions.

In those moments when they lack direction, Ding Hai individuals can all too easily be influenced by peer pressure. Rather than take the high road and stand alone, they may find it easier to "go with the flow". They may also find forms of escapism through trivial pursuits. This only scatters their energy and renders them ineffective.

When bored or under extreme emotional stress, Ding Hai individuals contemplate simply giving up, or sway towards the 'dark side'. They will resort to take shortcuts in life, even to the extent of using unconventional methods to reach their goals. This can be easily conquered through careful planning and by simply reminding themselves of the importance of perseverance and being mindful of their moral compass.

Key Character Traits of the Ding Hai 辛丑: Overall

- Intuitive
- Sensitive
- Idealistic
- Imaginative
- Intelligent
- Pragmatic
- Thirst for knowledge

Work Life

丁亥

Ding Hai

Professional Self

The Ding Hai uses work as an outlet for their energy and talents. It does not matter what profession or business they delve into because they will inevitably be successful at it.

Originality makes those born under this Pillar excellent strategists. Their innovation gives them much joy in initiating their own projects and allows them to make improvements in existing systems. Their inborn business skills, coupled with their intuition, also allow them to recognize financial opportunities before others.

Their inherent interest in others makes them ideal for humanitarian work. A humanitarian cause may also be the best outlet for their grand plans and original ideas. They also know instinctively how to network and are able to make the perfect contacts as needed.

Initially, their restlessness and impatience may prevent them from excelling, but once they apply themselves and focus on a job, they shine at it.

Career Options

Several career fields would match the many traits of Ding Hai individuals.

Their innate power of persuasion would make them perfectly suited for positions in advertising, media or publishing, while their drive for a worthy cause may push them into science, medicine or alternative healing.

Their keen organizational skills may draw them into the administration field. They will only want to stick with this field, however, if it involves a variety of individuals and projects.

This love for variety would make them best suited as financial advisors, mediators or negotiators. To capitalize on their love for people even more, they could consider becoming a teacher, trainer, agent, or propagandist. As Ding Hai individuals are charismatic and charming, they make good team leaders and motivational gurus.

On the other end of the career scale, they may choose to enter fields that involve interior design or style. They have an excellent eye for color and form and are pretty imaginative when putting it all together. These characteristics would make them an excellent painter as well.

If they pay attention to their flair for the dramatic, they may discover that their true desire may be in theater, music or acting.

Key Character Traits of the Ding Hai 丁亥: Work life

Positive

- Organized
- Enthusiastic
- Energetic
- Determined
- Optimistic

Negative

- Impatient
- Overbearing
- Egotistical
- Domineering
- Unfocused

Love and Relationships

丁亥

Ding Hai

Love

Ding Hai individuals are motivated to find their life partner. It takes time for them to fall in love, but once done, they work hard to remain committed and harmonious. This also means that they are very committed to a relationship and no work is too hard when it comes to building and sustaining the romantic flavor in a relationship.

The ideal partner for them is someone who is as strong and hardworking as they are. It would also be great if this person shared the same ideals as they do. Once they have found that person, no sacrifice is too great. In other words, matters of the heart deal importantly for them in life.

They are sensitive to others and may find themselves going through many changes in response to the needs of their partner. It is vital, however, that they retain their independence.

Acquaintances

Those born under this Pillar are sociable, charming and charismatic. Naturally friendly and diplomatic, they are able to attract many friends. They enjoy meeting new people and prefer the company of hardworking successful individuals who are also mentally stimulating. They are a go-to source for practical advice, which is why many are comfortable in their presence.

Sometimes their unsettled nature can put them at odds with others. If Ding Hai individuals do not experience exciting change in their friendship, they get stuck in a rut and become restless. Once they lose interest, they appear cold, aloof and abrupt. They might have to break out from their shell more often to seek new perspective and view.

Family

Maintaining unity within their family is important to the Ding Hai. They are hospitable and generous to all members of their family and their innate diplomatic skills help keep situations calm. They are also highly protective of their family and will defend loved ones to the fullest.

While it is easy for them to express their love and affection, tolerance is the key to a favorable marriage. Good communication is the base that fosters tolerance in a marriage. The Ding Hai must look into expressing their needs and wants as well, and getting to know their partner on a deeper level, as opposed to relying on affection and sweet nothings.

They should remember not to let their emotions become repressed. If this happens, they will become inconsiderate or willful towards their closest family members.

Key Character Traits of the Ding Hai 丁亥: Love & Relationships

- Protective
- Generous
- Charming
- Compassionate
- Empathetic

Famous Personalities

Anne Cox Chambers - American media proprietor and billionaire. She is the primary owner of Cox Enterprises, a privately owned media empire.

Philip Knight - American business magnate and philanthropist. He is the co-founder and chairman of Nike, Inc.

Charles R. Schwab - American businessman and investor. He is the founder of Charles Schwab Corporation, a brokerage and banking company.

Paul Tudor Jones II - American hedge fund manager and billionaire. He is the founder of Tudor Investment Corporation, a management company that handles his various investment partnerships.

Source: Wikipedia (June 2013)

Technical Analysis

丁亥

Ding Hai

BaZi Day Pillar Analytics 日柱分析

時 Hour	日 Day	月 Month	年 Year	
	丁 [日元 DM] Ding Yin Fire			天干 Heavenly Stems
	亥 [胎 Conceived] Hai Pig Yin Water			地支 Earthly Branches
	壬 Ren 甲 Jia + Water + Wood 官 DO 印 DR			藏干 Hidden Stems

八字一柱論命法

丁亥
Fire
Pig

The Direct Resource 正印星 and Officer 官星 Stars are hidden inside the Branch of this Ding Hai Pillar. The Officer 官星 and Resource 印星 Stars also seen to be produce each other. This represents intelligent and extremely talented individuals. The Ding Hai 丁亥 Pillar holds a 'hidden' combination between the Ding stem and Ren stem it sits on that attracts the influence of the Resource element. This denotes a highly intuitive and remarkably sharp witted individual. This Pillar also sits on the Nobleman Star 貴人星, which signifies that the Ding Hai will always attract the help of Noble, helpful mentors at their times of need. For female Ding Hai, it represents that they will marry a capable and loving husband.

Ding Hai individuals are naturally determined and extremely energetic. Assertive and courageous; they are always poised for action and will inspire others with their bravery, courage and enthusiasm in facing challenges

The BaZi 60 Pillars Life Analysis Method   291

head on. They are highly innovative and love to walk first into the unknown with a pioneering spirit. They are natural leaders and often have tremendous potential in influencing people.

The Ding Hai may find that they have two distinct sides to their personality. They can be practical and organized achievers and also restless and undisciplined dreamers. They can be optimistic and motivational or pessimistic and negative. They can be gregarious one moment and cold and uncaring the next. Their ambitious and enterprising nature often means that they are very independent, with a drive to strike out on their own, but they long to be part of a group and can be very dependent on their loved ones. They can be critical, stubborn, self-centered and a law unto themselves and they can also be receptive, intuitive and responsible.

The Ding Hai may sometimes need to learn to take a step back and to treat their companions with greater respect and consideration. It will often benefit them to develop a strong system of values and to use their intuition to enhance their own good judgment in dealing with their relationships and personal struggles. As they are very practical and have their feet planted firmly on the ground this should not be hard for them to do. The Ding Hai's boundless energy means that they always are likely to benefit from the support of their friends and admirers.

Technical Observations

The Ding Hai 丁亥 Pillar sits on a Traveling Star, indicative of frequent travel and mobility. This Pillar is considered as one of the Loyal Pillars, as it sits on the Direct Officer Star 正官星, which symbolizes good natured, cultured and educated individuals. There is also a hidden-pull combination of the Wu 午 (Horse). This suggests that there is a hidden 'attraction' to fans and friends towards this Day Pillar. Because inside the Wu 午(Horse) is the Friend Star 比肩星.

It is very favourable if this Pillar meets with the Ren Water 壬 Officer Star in the Chart or in the Luck Pillars as this combination is known as the Covered Lamp in the Palace 罩宮燈. This signifies superior academic achievements and breakthroughs as well as a highly successful life for this Ding Hai individual. It is also favourable for this Pillar to meet with the Geng 庚 at the Stems. This combination is known as the Control in Hands 墮鎮在手 formation. If the Ren 壬 is not present in this particular Chart, then the Jia 甲 will be clashed 冲 by the Geng 庚, which symbolizes potential bankruptcy and, in extreme cases serious accidents in life.

Those born in the Spring and Summer months have a greater chance to have good fortune in their career. Born in the Winter and Autumn months, they are better suited to working independently and do not rely on the help from others. Those born during the day time (5AM – 5PM) may expect to find fortune without abundant wealth. Those born at night time (5PM – 5AM) may gain greater success in life with the support of others.

It is not a favorable event to be born in the Chen 辰 (Dragon) month because it is indicative a life full of unforeseen challenges which inadvertently will impede the achievements for this individual.

Unique 60 Pillar Combinations

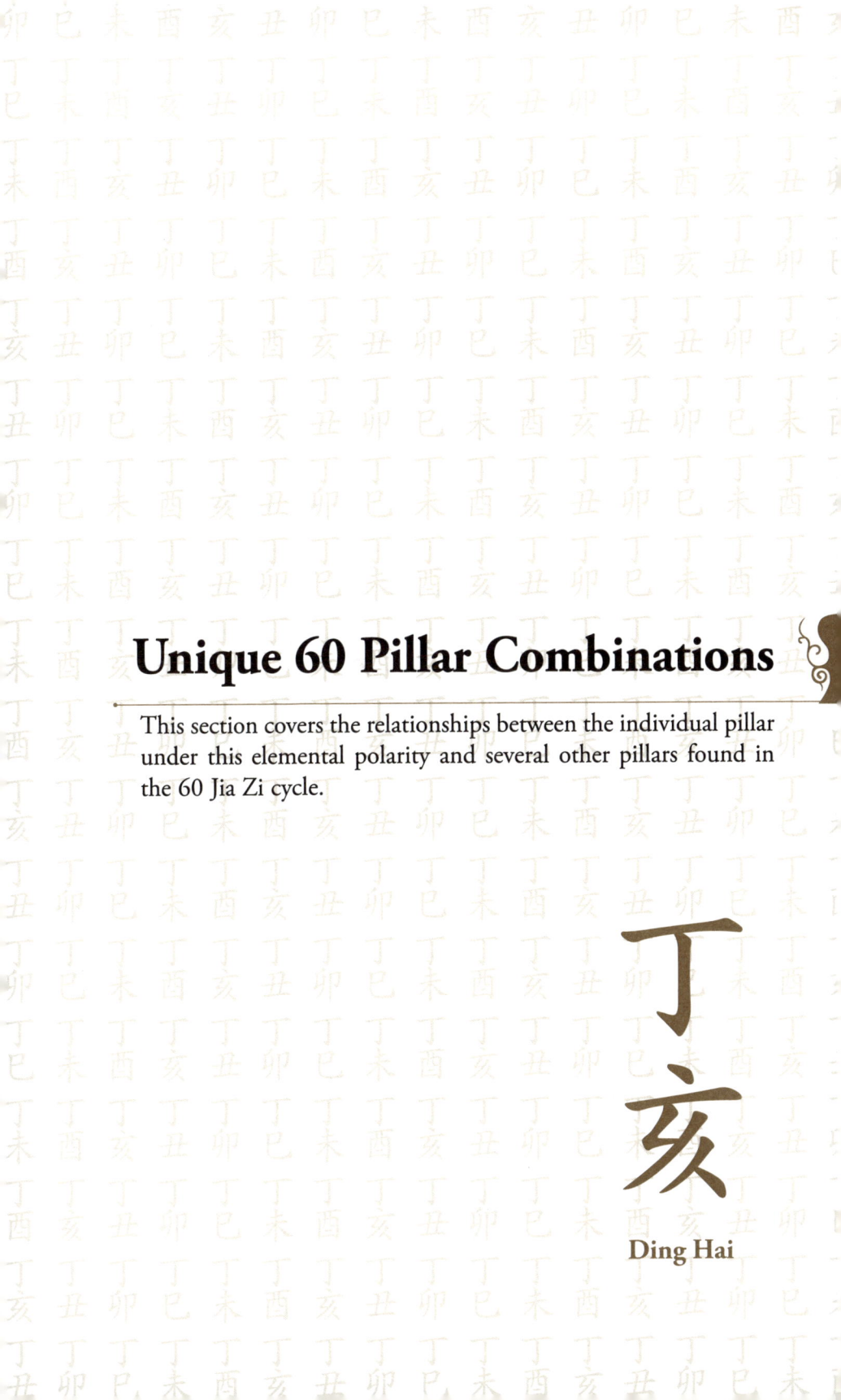

This section covers the relationships between the individual pillar under this elemental polarity and several other pillars found in the 60 Jia Zi cycle.

丁亥

Ding Hai

Heaven Combine Earth Harm 天合地害
Ding Hai 丁亥 (Fire Pig) + Ren Shen 壬申 (Water Monkey)

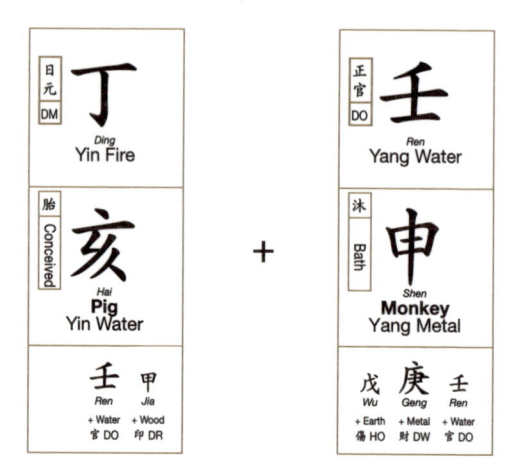

日元 DM — 丁 Ding Yin Fire	正官 DO — 壬 Ren Yang Water
胎 Conceived — 亥 Hai Pig Yin Water	沐 Bath — 申 Shen Monkey Yang Metal
壬 Ren +Water 官 DO / 甲 Jia +Wood 印 DR	戊 Wu +Earth 傷 HO / 庚 Geng +Metal 財 DW / 壬 Ren +Water 官 DO

In this configuration, the Heavenly Stem combines with the Earthly Branch to form a Harm 害. The symbolism represents a situation which appears positive due to the presence of the Heavenly Stem but includes underlying feelings of uncertainty, distrust and insecurity indicated by the formation of the Harm.

This can be found in the BaZi Natal Chart in the Year, Month and Hour Pillars as well as the Luck and Annual Pillars.

When found in the Year Pillar, the individual will appear to have a good relationship with their grandparents but there will be tensions beneath the surface and there will not be any trust in the relationship. As the Year Pillar also governs a person's social circle, this configuration here would indicate that the individual may be very detached in his/her friendships or is more of a loner who shies away from socializing.

Located in the Month Pillar, the same feelings and doubt and insecurity will be found in the relationship with the individual's parents, regardless of how positive the outward appearance may be. The Month Pillar also represents one's career and work life, and the configuration here means that the individual lacks affinity with his/her peers and superiors at work. Thus, this may eventually impede their career progression due to poor support from these people.

The Ding Hai individual is likely to have problems in their relationship with their children or with their employees, clients and suppliers if this configuration is found in the Hour Pillar. As the Hour Pillar also signifies one's hopes and dreams, this could denote a lost sense of direction or purpose in life for this individual.

When the Heaven Combine Earth Harm is located in the Luck Pillar, it suggests that though the Ding Hai may appear to be successful and on the surface their hopes and plans are coming to fruition they may nevertheless feel that these achievements have come at a cost and they may be left feeling abused or victimized. They may be left feeling merely exhausted by their exertions and fail to find any peace or satisfaction in their accomplishments.

Located in the Annual Pillar, this configuration represents a year that begins with a feeling of optimism but ends on a note of disappointment. This may be the result of jealousy however and the individual may find greater peace of mind if they can accept that what they have in enough and not compare themselves with others.

Heaven Friend Earth Clash 天比地冲
Ding Hai 丁亥 (Fire Pig) + Ding Si 丁巳 (Fire Snake)

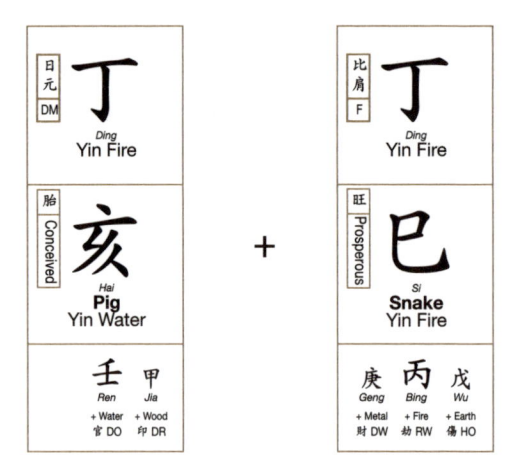

日元 DM	丁 Ding Yin Fire		比肩 F	丁 Ding Yin Fire
胎 Conceived	亥 Hai **Pig** Yin Water	+	旺 Prosperous	巳 Si **Snake** Yin Fire
壬 Ren +Water 官 DO	甲 Jia +Wood 印 DR		庚 Geng +Metal 财 DW	丙 Bing +Fire 劫 RW	戊 Wu +Earth 傷 HO

This configuration represents a promise that fails to live up to its expectation, or agreements that appear to progress smoothly at first but unexpectedly fall apart in the end. The Heaven Friend Earth Clash also indicates an appearance of being very busy with no time to spare, but in truth, the individual's frenetic endeavors do not amount to anything significant achieved.

The Heaven Friend Earth Clash indicates unanticipated events that may cause upset and dissatisfaction at first, but may ultimately prove to be good later. Whether the outcome is positive will depend on whether the Heavenly Stem is favorable or unfavorable.

This configuration can be found in the BaZi Natal Chart in the Year, Month and Hour Pillars as well as the Luck and Annual Pillars.

Found in the Year Pillar of the Natal Chart, the configuration is likely to have an impact on the individual's relationship with their grandparents. An unexpected turn could cause the relationship to change in some way. The Year Pillar also represents one's social circle, and the individual with this configuration here may have a distant relationship with his/her friends due to trust issues.

If this configuration is in the Month Pillar, the individual and their parents are likely to feel that their relationship is altered by unforeseen circumstances. This individual will have difficulty getting support or even trust from these parties and thus, causing them to be insecure as a result. As the Month Pillar governs one's work and career, the individual's relationship with his/her superiors and peers are poor due to gossips or office politics.

The same situation occurs when this configuration appears in the Hour Pillar of the Natal Chart - only this time with an impact on the individual's relationship with their children or with their employees and clients. This may lead to a lack of respect shown towards this individual. The Hour Pillar also governs one's hopes and dreams, and this could mean that the individual may find it challenging to achieve their goals.

When this configuration appears in the Luck Pillar, Ding Hai individuals can expect an incoming period of steady, if painful, change. Though it may not be apparent at the time this will be a time of growth and progression and the ultimate outcome will be a positive.

A year of surprise endings is in store when the Heaven Friend Earth Clash is found in the Ding Hai's Annual Pillar. Unanticipated twists and turns will characterize the year but it will also be one of self-discovery. The individual will learn and grow as a person through their experiences.

Heaven Friend Earth Punish 天比地刑
Ding Hai 丁亥 (Fire Pig) + Ding Hai 丁亥 (Wood Pig)

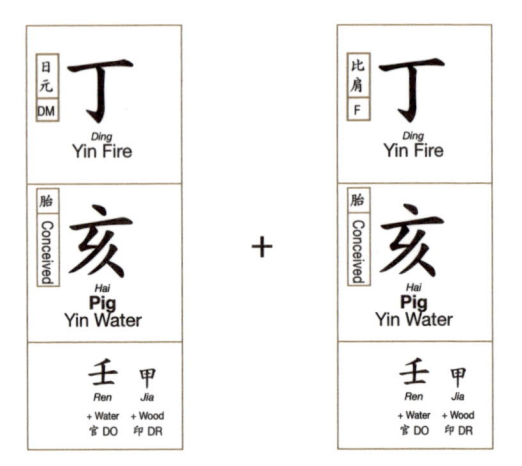

This configuration, though similar to the Heaven Combine Earth Punish, is unique because it doesn't form a combination. Instead the appearance of the Friend Star 比肩星 in the Stem indicates that the Self faces personal battles and psychological growth as the dominant themes of the Pillar.

The Earthly Branch forms a Punishment 刑 which is an indication of emotional pain and inner tension as well as stress but due to theme of this Pillar a lot of these emotions may be self-inflicted.

The Heaven Friend Earth Punish may be found in the BaZi Natal Chart in the Year, Month, or Hour Pillars as well as the Luck and Annual Pillars.

When located in the Year Pillar, the individual will maintain the façade of a positive relationship with their grandparents but they will be insecure and afraid that they cannot live up to their grandparents' expectations. They may not have the confidence to feeling be themselves in their company.

Similarly, the Heaven Friend Earth Punish in the Month indicates that the individual is likely to feel inadequate and unable to fulfill their parents' hopes and dreams for them. Their parents may have full confidence in them but this will not change how they feel. A position here may also have an impact on the individual's professional life and it could be an indication they are experiencing some work related stress. This could be to do with relationships at work; they may not have much faith in their colleagues and may feel overburdened. Some of the fault may rest with the individual however and they may need to address their own emotional state before they will be able to find a resolution.

When the configuration is found in the Hour Pillar, they may worry that they are failing in their role as parents. The relationship may well appear to be a close one and the children may be very happy but the Ding Hai will nevertheless fear that they are unable to offer enough emotional or material support.

Should this configuration appear in the Luck Pillar, it indicates a period of obstacles and setbacks. The individual may feel that their pride or confidence is wounded as they may face some tough challenges. Their relationships may come under some strain and they will need to be patient and trusting with their loved ones. Ultimately this will be a time of learning.

When the Heaven Friend Earth Punish is located in the Annual Pillar, the Ding Hai is likely to be lured into affairs or flirtatious relationship that could result in the individual to be distracted from their careers with a potentially negative impact.

Heaven and Earth Clash 天冲地冲
Ding Hai 丁亥 (Fire Pig) + Gui Si 癸巳 (Water Snake)

丁 Ding — 日元 DM — Yin Fire
亥 Hai — 胎 Conceived — Pig, Yin Water
 - 壬 Ren +Water 官 DO
 - 甲 Jia +Wood 印 DR

癸 Gui — 七殺 7K — Yin Water
巳 Si — 旺 Prosperous — Snake, Yin Fire
 - 庚 Geng +Metal 財 DW
 - 丙 Bing +Fire 劫 RW
 - 戊 Wu +Earth 傷 HO

The Heaven and Earth Clash formation has the effect of drainage on the individual's Day Pillar where its positive qualities are diminished. Also called the Fan Yin 反吟 or the unlucky formation, it is often also an indication of obstacles and setbacks.

Individuals connected to the Ding Hai who have this Pillar in their charts may also prove to be a negative influence. Though they may have only the Ding Hai's best interests at heart they could give poor advice and lead them astray.

The Heaven and Earth Clash can be found in the Year, Month and Hour Pillars as well as the Luck and Annual Pillars.

When it is encountered in the Year Pillar, the individual is likely to feel a lack of affinity with their grandparents. This may be because this individual feels detached and is unable to relate to them, and therefore could not establish closer ties with them. The same can be said about the individual and the relationship with their close friends as the Year Pillar also governs one's social circle.

In the Month Pillar, this configuration indicates the individual will have a distant or difficult relationship with their parents, which could probably stem from misunderstandings or miscommunications. As the Month Pillar also represents work and career, this configuration reflects the sour affinity between the individual and their colleagues and employers. This leads to a lack of support and recognition at work for this individual.

When found in the Hour Pillar, the individual may struggle to connect with their children. This is likely due to the individual inability to relate to their children. This individual is advised to make efforts to spend some quality time with their children to nurture a better bond. The Hour Pillar also represents one's ideas and hopes. The individual may have a hard time getting his/her ideas accepted or that he/she may lose sight of their purpose in life.

The outlook is no better when this arrangement is located in the Luck Pillar. This unlucky formation indicates a tumultuous time in which the individual will face obstacles, challenges and disappointments. However, this individual must not lose hope and see this experience as something that will make him/her stronger and more able to handle anything in the future.

If this configuration appears in the Annual Pillar, the individual is advised not to make any change or investment that may have serious ramifications. They are advised to maintain a low profile. They should use this time instead for personal development, in preparation to embrace new opportunities ahead when this period is over.

Heaven Counter Earth Clash 天剋地沖
Ding Hai 丁亥 (Fire Pig) + Xin Si 辛巳 (Metal Snake)

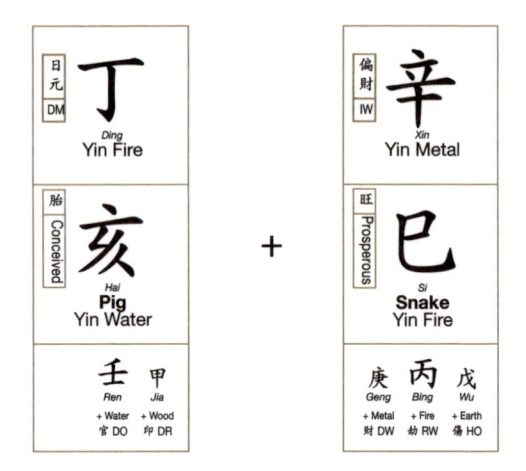

日元 DM	丁 Ding Yin Fire
胎 Conceived	亥 Hai Pig Yin Water

	壬 Ren +Water 官 DO	甲 Jia +Wood 印 DR

\+

偏財 IW	辛 Xin Yin Metal
旺 Prosperous	巳 Si Snake Yin Fire

庚 Geng +Metal 財 DW	丙 Bing +Fire 劫 RW	戊 Wu +Earth 傷 HO

Not to be confused with the Heaven and Earth Clash, which acts to negate the positive qualities of the individual's Pillar, the Heaven Counter Earth Clash formation places them firmly in control and gives them a passionate desire to succeed at any cost. These individuals are likely to be dominant characters, they may be forceful and impatient, they may have to guard against being over hasty at times, but ultimately they will be winners. People with this configuration in their chart often have an entrepreneurial flair and it is considered to be a good indication of wealth and achievement.

This configuration may be found in the BaZi Natal Chart in the Year, Month and Hour Pillars as well as in the Luck and Annual Pillars.

When located in the Year Pillar, it is an indication that the Ding Hai individual may have influential friends. These individuals may act as advisors or even investors in their projects.

A keen business sense is implied when the Heaven Counter Earth Clash appears in the Month Pillar. They are likely to be good with numbers and are adept in generating profits for their business.

The potentially negative impact of this configuration can be seen in the Hour Pillar. In this position may allow their passion to become an obsession. They are likely to be workaholics who will not make time for their families or personal relationships.

When the Heaven Counter Earth Clash Pillar is in the Luck Pillar the individual will feel the financial benefits of a myriad of new business opportunities.

A position in the Annual Pillar is also an indication of opportunity and business success. The individual is likely to advance in their careers and reap the financial rewards but they are also likely to be placed under some significant stress and their personal lives will feel the strain.

Heaven and Earth Unity 天同地比
Ding Hai 丁亥 (Fire Pig) + Ding Hai 丁亥 (Wood Pig)

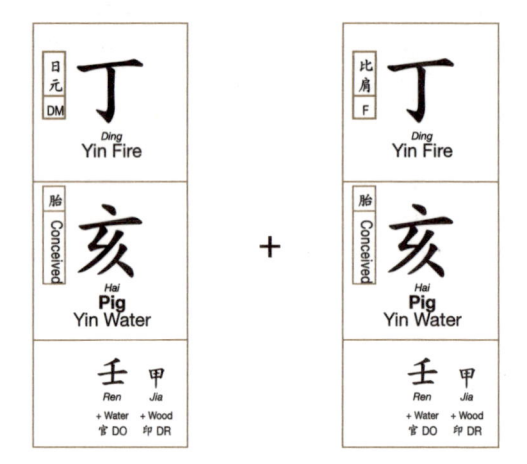

This arrangement has traditionally been called the Fu Yin 伏吟 which is known as the Hidden Warning Pillar. This configuration indicates sorrow and emotionally upsetting events. In certain circumstances, this formation is also known as the Heaven Friend Earth Punish configuration, depending on the overall view of the BaZi Chart.

It can be found in the BaZi Natal Chart in the Year, Month and Hour Pillars and in the Luck and Annual Pillars.

When found in the Year Pillar, it may indicate that the individual will have a weak or distant relationship with their grandparents. It may be that they have never even met their grandparents, even if they probably live close by.

When it is located in the Month Pillar, this configuration is an indication of a strained or severed bond with the individual's parents. They may struggle to connect with their parents in any significant way. This could also point to issues with regard to inheritance or a family business.

In the Hour Pillar, this configuration indicates that the individual may not have a desirable closeness with their children. Their children may live separately to them or have been raised by their grandparents. It may also be an indication of problems with fertility.

When located in the Luck Pillar, this configuration implies the individual will choose to live a very religious path. Spirituality is likely to have great significance for them even if it does not become a vocation. Alternatively they may focus on their body as a temple and become preoccupied with matters pertaining to their health. The presence of this Pillar may also indicate that they will suffer a loss of one of their parents.

When this arrangement appears in the Annual Pillar, the Ding Hai is likely to achieve a great deal. They will advance in their careers and see an increase in their material wealth. They may invest in property. However lurking behind this success will be at least one emotionally draining or stressful event which will overshadow the year.

Heaven and Earth Combo 天地相合
Ding Hai 丁亥 (Fire Pig) + Ren Yin 壬寅 (Water Tiger)

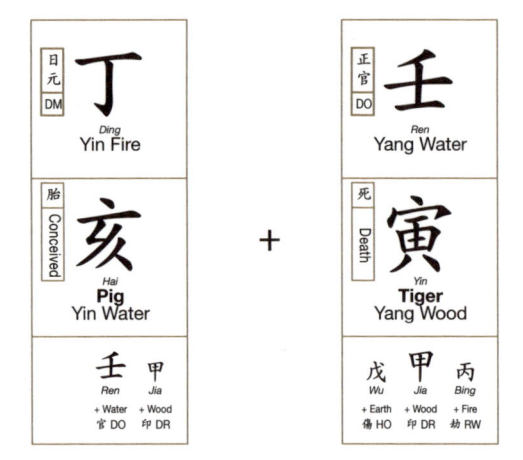

日元 DM	**Ding** Yin Fire 丁		正官 DO	**Ren** Yang Water 壬
胎 Conceived	**Hai** Pig Yin Water 亥	**+**	死 Death	**Yin** Tiger Yang Wood 寅
	壬 Ren +Water 官 DO　甲 Jia +Wood 印 DR			戊 Wu +Earth 傷 HO　甲 Jia +Wood 印 DR　丙 Bing +Fire 劫 RW

This configuration is, without a doubt, the most fortunate to see in a BaZi chart. It represents exceptional relationships in all areas of the individual's life bringing success and happiness with them.

When this configuration is present in the chart of one connected to the Ding Hai, it is an indication that these two will have a particular connection, this person is also like to be a positive influence and they are likely to be able to offer help and support in times of need.

When it arises in the Year Pillar, this configuration indicates that the individual will be very close to their grandparents. They also likely to be very popular and have strong bonds with their friends which will mean they will enjoy good social status.

The individual will have a great rapport with their parents when the configuration is located in the Month Pillar. They are also likely to benefit from the respect and appreciation of those in authority at work. As such, career progression is possibly smooth.

When the Heaven and Earth Combine configuration is located in the Hour Pillar, the individual will be blessed with a warm and loving bond with their children. They are also likely to be well regarded by their employees and clients.

A presence in the Luck and Annual Pillars is an indication that the individual will benefit from successful relationship in all areas of their life. They will be lucky in love and close with their families. They are also likely to prosper though joint ventures and working partnerships.

Rob Wealth Goat Blade 劫財羊刃
Ding Hai 丁亥 (Fire Pig) + Bing Wu 丙午 (Fire Horse)

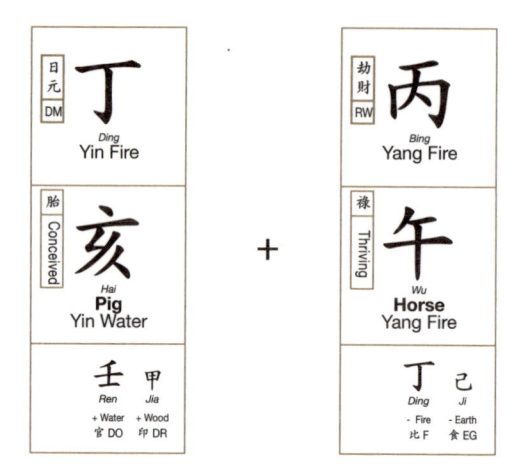

日元 DM	Ding 丁 Yin Fire
胎 Conceived	Hai 亥 Pig Yin Water

Ren 壬 +Water 官 DO
Jia 甲 +Wood 印 DR

劫財 RW	Bing 丙 Yang Fire
祿 Thriving	Wu 午 Horse Yang Fire

Ding 丁 −Fire 比 F
Ji 己 −Earth 食 EG

The Rob Wealth Goat Blade 劫財羊刃 formation is an indication of financial losses and potentially also of relationship problems. This configuration may have an impact on the Ding Hai even if it found in the Charts of those close to them. These individuals may somehow be the cause of them losing money. This may not be due to any ill-doing on their part and it may not even be noticed at the time. They may give poor career or investment advice. Or they could simply be a catalyst for the Ding Hai to overspend.

About Joey Yap

Joey Yap first began learning about Chinese Metaphysics from masters in the field when he was fifteen.

Despite having graduated with a Commerce degree in Accounting, Joey never became an accountant. Instead, he began to give seminars, talks and professional Chinese Metaphysic consultations in Malaysia, Singapore, India, Australia, Canada, England, Germany and the United States, becoming a household name in the field.

By the age of twenty-six, Joey became a self-made millionaire and in 2008, he was listed in The Malaysian Tatler as the Top 300 Most Influential People in Malaysia and Prestige's Top 40 Under 40.

His practical and result-driven take on Feng Shui and BaZi sets him apart from other older, traditional masters and practitioners in the field. He shows people how the ancient teachings can be utilized for tangible REAL world benefits. The success he and his clients enjoy, thanks to his advice, is positive proof that Feng Shui and BaZi Astrology works, whether everyone believes in it or not!

Today, Joey has helped and worked with governments and the wealthiest people in Singapore, Hong Kong, China, Malaysia and Japan. His clients include multinationals, developers, tycoons and royalties. On Bloomberg, he is featured on-air as a regular guest on the subject of Feng Shui annual forecasts. He is retained by twenty-five top Malaysian property developers to help determine suitable candidates to take top management, change their space and Feng Shui mechanism, the way they make decisions, and understand the natural cosmic energies that can influence their decision-making.

Joey is devoted to using his success to advance the field he works within.

The Joey Yap Consulting Group is the world's largest and first specialized metaphysics consultation firm. His consultancy, and professional speaking and training engagements with Microsoft, HP, Bloomberg, Citibank, HSBC and many more have seen the benefits of Classical Feng Shui and BaZi find their way into corporate environment and culture. Celebrities, property developers and other large organizations turn to Joey when they need the best.

After years of field-testing and fine-tuning his teachings, he has put together a team in the form of Joey Yap Research International. The objective of this Research Team is to scientifically track and verify the positive impact of Feng

Shui and BaZi on subjects and ultimately to assist more people in achieving their life goals.

The Mastery Academy of Chinese Metaphysics which Joey founded teaches thousands of students from all around the world about Classical Feng Shui, Chinese Astrology and Face Reading. Many graduates have gone on to become successful in their own right, becoming sought after consultants, setting up their own consultancy businesses or even becoming educators, passing on Chinese Metaphysics knowledge to others.

Joey has also created the Decision Referential Technology™, offering decision reformation training on how to make better decisions in business and in personal life. He has led his team of highly trained consultants to help clients create more positive change in corporate boardrooms and increase production in their companies, helping people see their business outlook for each year so they may anticipate, plan and execute their strategies successfully.

Joey's work has been featured regularly in various popular global publications and networks like Time, Forbes, the International Herald Tribune and Bloomberg. He has also written columns for The New Straits Times, The Star and The Edge – Malaysia's leading newspapers.

He has achieved bestselling author status with over 85 books, on Feng Shui, Chinese Astrology (BaZi), Face Reading and Yi Jing, which has sold more than three million copies to-date. Many of his titles have also topped the Malaysian and Singaporean MPH Bookstores' bestseller lists.

It is safe to say that Joey Yap is a world leader in the field of Chinese Metaphysics.

His success is not limited to matters of Feng Shui and BaZi. Although his success is a product of them, he is also a successful entrepreneur, leading his own companies and property investment portfolio. When not teaching metaphysics or consulting around the world, Joey is a Naruto fan, avid snowboarder and is crazy for fruits de mer.

Author's personal website :

www.joeyyap.com

Joey Yap on Facebook:

www.facebook.com/JoeyYapFB

www.masteryacademy.com | +603 - 2284 8080

MASTERY ACADEMY
OF CHINESE METAPHYSICS
Your **Preferred** Choice to the Art & Science of Classical Chinese Metaphysics Studies

Bringing **innovative** techniques and **creative** teaching methods to an ancient study.

Mastery Academy of Chinese Metaphysics was established by Joey Yap to play the role of disseminating this Eastern knowledge to the modern world with the belief that this valuable knowledge should be accessible to anyone, anywhere.

Its goal is to enrich people's lives through accurate, professional teaching and practice of Chinese Metaphysics knowledge globally. It is the first academic institution of its kind in the world to adopt the tradition of Western institutions of higher learning - where students are encourage to explore, question and challenge themselves and to respect different fields and branches of study - with the appreciation and respect of classical ideas and applications that have stood the test of time.

The art and science of Chinese Metaphysics studies – be it Feng Shui, BaZi (Astrology), Mian Xiang (Face Reading), ZeRi (Date Selection) or Yi Jing – is no longer a field shrouded with mystery and superstition. In light of new technology, fresher interpretations and innovative methods as well as modern teaching tools like the Internet, interactive learning, e-learning and distance learning, anyone from virtually any corner of the globe, who is keen to master these disciplines can do so with ease and confidence under the guidance and support of the Academy.

It has indeed proven to be a center of educational excellence for thousands of students from over thirty countries across the world; many of whom have moved on to practice classical Chinese Metaphysics professionally in their home countries.

At the Academy, we believe in enriching people's lives by empowering their destinies through the disciplines of Chinese Metaphysics. Learning is not an option - it's a way of life!

MALAYSIA
19-3, The Boulevard, Mid Valley City, 59700 Kuala Lumpur, Malaysia
Tel : +603-2284 8040 | Fax : +603-2284 1218
Email   : info@masteryacademy.com
Website : www.masteryacademy.com

Australia, Austria, Canada, China, Croatia, Cyprus, Czech Republic, Denmark, France, Germany, Greece, Hungary, India, Italy, Kazakhstan, Malaysia, Netherlands (Holland), New Zealand, Philippines, Poland, Russian Federation, Singapore, Slovenia, South Africa, Switzerland, Turkey, U.S.A., Ukraine, United Kingdom

www.masteryacademy.com | +603 - 2284 8080

Mastery Academy around the world

www.masteryacademy.com | +603 - 2284 8080

JOEY YAP CONSULTING GROUP

Pioneering Metaphysics - Centric Personal Coaching and Corporate Consulting

The Joey Yap Consulting Group is the world's first specialised metaphysics consultation firm. Founded in 2002 by renown international Feng Shui and BaZi consultant, author and trainer Joey Yap, the Joey Yap Consulting Group is a pioneer in the provision of metaphysics-driven coaching and consultation services for individuals and corporations.

The Group's core consultation practice areas are Feng Shui and BaZi, which are complimented by ancillary services like Date Selection, Face Reading and Yi Jing Divination. The Group's team of highly-trained professional consultants are led by Principal Consultant Joey Yap. The Joey Yap Consulting Group is the firm of choice for corporate captains, entrepreneurs, celebrities and property developers when it comes to Feng Shui and BaZi-related advisory and knowledge.

Across Industries: Our Portfolio of Clients

Our diverse portfolio of both corporate and individual clients from all around the world bears testimony to our experience and capabilities.

Joey Yap Consulting Group is the firm of choice for many of Asia's leading multi-national corporations, listed entities, conglomerates and top-tier property developers when it comes to Feng Shui and corporate BaZi.

Our services also engaged by professionals, prominent business personalities, celebrities, high-profile politicians and people from all walks of life.

JOEY YAP CONSULTING GROUP

Name (Mr./Mrs./Ms.):_____

Contact Details

Tel:_____ Fax:_____

Mobile :_____

E-mail:_____

What Type of Consultation Are You Interested In?
☐ Feng Shui ☐ BaZi ☐ Date Selection ☐ Corporate Events

Please tick if applicable:
☐ Are you a Property Developer looking to engage Joey Yap Consulting Group?

☐ Are you a Property Investor looking for tailor-made packages to suit your investment requirements?

Please attach your name card here.

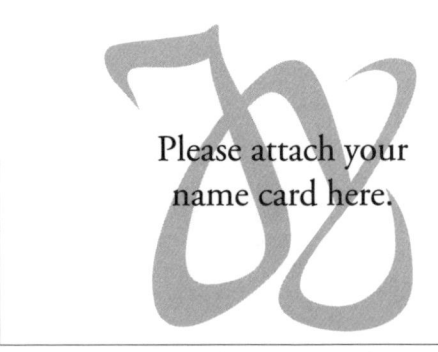

Thank you for completing this form. Please fax it back to us at:

Malaysia & the rest of the world
Fax : +603-2284 2213   Tel : +603-2284 1213

www.joeyyap.com

www.joeyyap.com

Feng Shui Consultations

For Residential Properties
- Initial Land/Property Assessment
- Residential Feng Shui Consultations
- Residential Land Selection
- End-to-End Residential Consultation

For Commercial Properties
- Initial Land/Property Assessment
- Commercial Feng Shui Consultations
- Commercial Land Selection
- End-to-End Commercial Consultation

For Property Developers
- End-to-End Consultation
- Post-Consultation Advisory Services
- Panel Feng Shui Consultant

For Property Investors
- Your Personal Feng Shui Consultant
- Tailor-Made Packages

For Memorial Parks & Burial Sites
- Yin House Feng Shui

BaZi Consultations

Personal Destiny Analysis
- Personal Destiny Analysis for Individuals
- Children's BaZi Analysis
- Family BaZi Analysis

Strategic Analysis for Corporate Organizations
- Corporate BaZi Consultations
- BaZi Analysis for Human Resource Management

Entrepreneurs & Business Owners
- BaZi Analysis for Entrepreneurs

Career Pursuits
- BaZi Career Analysis

Relationships
- Marriage and Compatibility Analysis
- Partnership Analysis

For Everyone
- Annual BaZi Forecast
- Your Personal BaZi Coach

Date Selection Consultations

- Marriage Date Selection
- Caesarean Birth Date Selection
- House-Moving Date Selection
- Renovation & Groundbreaking Dates
- Signing of Contracts
- Official Openings
- Product Launches

Corporate Events

Many reputable organizations and instituitions have worked closely with Joey Yap Consulting Group to build a synergistic business relationship by engaging our team of consultants, led by Joey Yap, as speakers at their corporate events.

We tailor our seminars and talks to suit the anticipated or pertinent group of audience. Be it department, subsidiary, your clients or even the entire corporation, we aim to fit your requirements in delivering the intended message(s).

Tel: +603-2284 1213   Email: consultation@joeyyap.com

CHINESE METAPHYSICS REFERENCE SERIES

The Chinese Metaphysics Reference Series is a collection of reference texts, source material, and educational textbooks to be used as supplementary guides by scholars, students, researchers, teachers and practitioners of Chinese Metaphysics.

These comprehensive and structured books provide fast, easy reference to aid in the study and practice of various Chinese Metaphysics subjects including Feng Shui, BaZi, Yi Jing, Zi Wei, Liu Ren, Ze Ri, Ta Yi, Qi Men and Mian Xiang.

The Chinese Metaphysics Compendium

At over 1,000 pages, the *Chinese Metaphysics Compendium* is a unique one-volume reference book that compiles ALL the formulas relating to Feng Shui, BaZi (Four Pillars of Destiny), Zi Wei (Purple Star Astrology), Yi Jing (I-Ching), Qi Men (Mystical Doorways), Ze Ri (Date Selection), Mian Xiang (Face Reading) and other sources of Chinese Metaphysics.

It is presented in the form of easy-to-read tables, diagrams and reference charts, all of which are compiled into one handy book. This first-of-its-kind compendium is presented in both English and the original Chinese, so that none of the meanings and contexts of the technical terminologies are lost.

The only essential and comprehensive reference on Chinese Metaphysics, and an absolute must-have for all students, scholars, and practitioners of Chinese Metaphysics.

The Ten Thousand Year Calendar (Pocket Edition)	The Ten Thousand Year Calendar	Dong Gong Date Selection	The Date Selection Compendium
Plum Blossoms Divination Reference Book	Xuan Kong Da Gua Ten Thousand Year Calendar	San Yuan Dragon Gate Eight Formations Water Method	
Bazi Hour Pillar Useful Gods - Wood	Bazi Hour Pillar Useful Gods - Fire	Bazi Hour Pillar Useful Gods - Earth	Bazi Hour Pillar Useful Gods - Metal
Bazi Hour Pillar Useful Gods - Water	Xuan Kong Da Gua Structures Reference Book		
Bazi Structures and Structural Useful Gods - Wood	Bazi Structures and Structural Useful Gods - Fire	Bazi Structures and Structural Useful Gods - Earth	Bazi Structures and Structural Useful Gods - Metal
Bazi Structures and Structural Useful Gods - Water	Xuan Kong Da Gua 64 Gua Transformation Analysis		
Earth Study Discern Truth Second Edition	Eight Mansions Bright Mirror	Secret of Xuan Kong	Ode to Flying Stars
Xuan Kong Purple White Script	Ode to Mysticism	The Yin House Handbook	

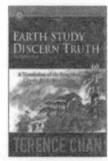

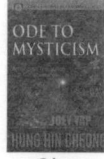

www.masteryacademy.com | +603 - 2284 8080

Joey Yap's BaZi Profiling System

Three Levels of BaZi Profiling (English & Chinese versions)

In BaZi Profiling, there are three levels that reflect three different stages of a person's personal nature and character structure.

Level 1 – The Day Master

The Day Master in a nutshell is the BASIC YOU. The inborn personality. It is your essential character. It answers the basic question "WHO AM I". There are ten basic personality profiles – the TEN Day Masters – each with its unique set of personality traits, likes and dislikes.

Level 2 – The Structure

The Structure is your behavior and attitude – in other words, how you use your personality. It expands on the Day Master (Level 1). The structure reveals your natural tendencies in life – are you more controlling, more of a creator, supporter, thinker or connector? Each of the Ten Day Masters express themselves differently through the FIVE Structures. Why do we do the things we do? Why do we like the things we like? – The answers are in our BaZi STRUCTURE.

Level 3 – The Profile

The Profile reveals your unique abilities and skills, the masks that you consciously and unconsciously "put on" as you approach and navigate the world. Your Profile speaks of your ROLES in life. There are TEN roles – or Ten BaZi Profiles. Everyone plays a different role.

What makes you happy and what does success mean to you is different to somebody else. Your sense of achievement and sense of purpose in life is unique to your Profile. Your Profile will reveal your unique style.

The path of least resistance to your success and wealth can only be accessed once you get into your "flow." Your BaZi Profile reveals how you can get FLOW. It will show you your patterns in work, relationship and social settings. Being AWARE of these patterns is your first step to positive Life Transformation.

www.baziprofiling.com

www.masteryacademy.com | +603 - 2284 8080

BaZi Collection

Leading Chinese Astrology Master Trainer Joey Yap makes it easy to learn how to unlock your Destiny through your BaZi with these books. BaZi or Four Pillars of Destiny is an ancient Chinese science which enables individuals to understand their personality, hidden talents and abilities as well as their luck cycle, simply by examining the information contained within their birth data.

Understand and appreciate more about this astoundingly accurate ancient Chinese Metaphysical science with this BaZi Collection.

If the Shoe Fits

This book is for the ones who want to make the effort to enhance their relationship. Yes, you read it right - EFFORT.

Hence, in her debut release, Jessie Lee humbly shares with you the classical BaZi method of the 10 Day Masters, and the combination of the new-founded profiling system developed by Joey Yap, to understand and to deal with the people around you.

Feng Shui Collection

Must-Haves for Property Analysis!

For homeowners, those looking to build their own home or even investors who are looking to apply Feng Shui to their homes, these series of books provides valuable information from the classical Feng Shui therioes and applications.

In his trademark straight-to-the-point manner, Joey shares with you the Feng Shui do's and dont's when it comes to finding a property with favorable Feng Shui, which is condusive for home living.

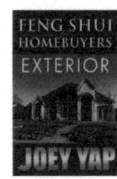

Stories & Lessons on Feng Shui Series

All in all, this series is a delightful chronicle of Joey's articles, thoughts and vast experience - as a professional Feng Shui consultant and instructor - that have been purposely refined, edited and expanded upon to make for a light-hearted, interesting yet educational read. And with Feng Shui, BaZi, Mian Xiang and Yi Jing all thrown into this one dish, there's something for everyone.

www.masteryacademy.com | +603 - 2284 8080

More Titles under Joey Yap Books

Pure Feng Shui

Pure Feng Shui is Joey Yap's debut with an international publisher, CICO Books, and is a refreshing and elegant look at the intricacies of Classical Feng Shui – now compiled in a useful manner for modern-day readers. This book is a comprehensive introduction to all the important precepts and techniques of Feng Shui practice.

Your Aquarium Here

This book is the first in Fengshuilogy Series, a series of matter-in-fact and useful Feng Shui books designed for the person who wants to do a fuss-free Feng Shui.

Xuan Kong Flying Stars

This book is an essential introductory book to the subject of Xuan Kong Fei Xing, a well-known and popular system of Feng Shui. Learn 'tricks of the trade' and 'trade secrets' to enhance and maximize Qi in your home or office.

Walking the Dragons

Compiled in one book for the first time from Joey Yap's Feng Shui Mastery Excursion Series, the book highlights China's extensive, vibrant history with astute observations on the Feng Shui of important sites and places. Learn the landform formations of Yin Houses (tombs and burial places), as well as mountains, temples, castles, and villages.

The Art of Date Selection: Personal Date Selection

With the *Art of Date Selection: Personal Date Selection*, learn simple, practical methods you can employ to select not just good dates, but personalized good dates. Whether it's a personal activity such as a marriage or professional endeavor such as launching a business, signing a contract or even acquiring assets, this book will show you how to pick the good dates and tailor them to suit the activity in question, as well as avoid the negative ones too!

Your Head Here

Your Head Here is the first book by Sherwin Ng, an accomplished student of Joey Yap, and an experienced Feng Shui consultant and instructor with Joey Yap Consulting Group and Mastery Academy respectively. Being the second book under the Fengshuilogy series, Your Head Here focuses on Bedroom Feng Shui, a specific topic dedicated to optimum bed location and placement.

Xuan Kong Nine Life Star series

Joey Yap's Feng Shui Essentials - Xuan Kong Nine Life Star series of books comprise nine individual titles that provide detailed information about each individual Life Star.

Based on the complex and highly-evolved Xuan Kong Feng Shui system, each book focuses on a particular Life Star and provides you with a detailed Feng Shui guide.

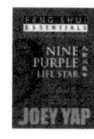

www.masteryacademy.com | +603 - 2284 8080

Face Reading Collection

Discover Face Reding (English & Chinese versions)

This is a comprehensive book on all areas of Face Reading, covering some of the most important facial features, including the forehead, mouth, ears and even philtrum above your lips. This book eill help you analyse not just your Destiny but help you achieve your full potential and achieve life fulfillment.

Joey Yap's Art of Face Reading

The Art of Face Reading is Joey Yap's second effort with CICO Books, and takes a lighter, more practical approach to Face Reading. This book does not so much focus on the individual features as it does on reading the entire face. It is about identifying common personality types and characters.

Faces of Fortune: The 20 Tycoons to bet on over the next 10 years

Faces of Fortune is Tee Lin Say's first book on the subject of Mian Xiang or Chinese Face Reading. As an accomplished Face Reading student of Joey Yap and an experienced business journalist, Lin Say merged both her knowledge into this volume, profiling twenty prominent tycoons in Asia based on the art of Face Reading.

Easy Guide on Face Reading (English & Chinese versions)

The Face Reading Essentials series of books comprises 5 individual books on the key features of the face – Eyes, Eyebrows, Ears, Nose, and Mouth. Each book provides a detailed illustration and a simple yet descriptive explanation on the individual types of the features.

The books are equally useful and effective for beginners, enthusiasts, and the curious. The series is designed to enable people who are new to Face Reading to make the most of first impressions and learn to apply Face Reading skills to understand the personality and character of friends, family, co-workers, and even business associates.

Annual Releases
2013 Annual Outlook & Tong Shu

| Chinese Astrology for 2013 | Feng Shui for 2013 | Tong Shu Desktop Calendar 2013 | Professional Tong Shu Diary 2013 | Tong Shu Monthly Planner 2013 | Weekly Tong Shu Diary 2013 |

www.masteryacademy.com | +603 - 2284 8080

Educational Tools and Software

Xuan Kong Flying Stars Feng Shui Software
The Essential Application for Enthusiasts and Professionals

The Xuan Kong Flying Stars Feng Shui Software will assist you in the practice of Xuan Kong Feng Shui with minimum fuss and maximum effectiveness. Superimpose the Flying Stars charts over your house plans (or those of your clients) to clearly demarcate the 9 Palaces. Use it to help you create fast and sophisticated chart drawings and presentations, as well as to assist professional practitioners in the report-writing process before presenting the final reports for your clients. Students can use it to practice their Xuan Kong Feng Shui skills and knowledge, and it can even be used by designers and architects!

BaZi Ming Pan Software Version 2.0
Professional Four Pillars Calculator for Destiny Analysis

The BaZi Ming Pan Version 2.0 Professional Four Pillars Calculator for Destiny Analysis is the most technically advanced software of its kind in the world today. It allows even those without any knowledge of BaZi to generate their own BaZi Charts, and provides virtually every detail required to undertake a comprehensive Destiny Analysis.

This Professional Four Pillars Calculator allows you to even undertake a day-to-day analysis of your Destiny. What's more, all BaZi Charts generated by this software are fully printable and configurable! Designed for both enthusiasts and professional practitioners, this state-of-the-art software blends details with simplicity, and is capable of generating 4 different types of BaZi charts: **BaZi Professional Charts, BaZi Annual Analysis Charts, BaZi Pillar Analysis Charts and BaZi Family Relationship Charts.**

Joey Yap Feng Shui Template Set

Directions are the cornerstone of any successful Feng Shui audit or application. The **Joey Yap Feng Shui Template Set** is a set of three templates to simplify the process of taking directions and determining locations and positions, whether it's for a building, a house, or an open area such as a plot of land, all with just a floor plan or area map.

The Set comprises 3 basic templates: The Basic Feng Shui Template, 8 Mansions Feng Shui Template, and the Flying Stars Feng Shui Template.

www.masteryacademy.com | +603 - 2284 8080

Educational Tools and Software

Xuan Kong Vol.1
An Advanced Feng Shui Home Study Course

Learn the Xuan Kong Flying Star Feng Shui system in just 20 lessons! Joey Yap's specialised notes and course work have been written to enable distance learning without compromising on the breadth or quality of the syllabus. Learn at your own pace with the same material students in a live class would use. The most comprehensive distance learning course on Xuan Kong Flying Star Feng Shui in the market. Xuan Kong Flying Star Vol.1 comes complete with a special binder for all your course notes.

Discover Feng Shui with Joey Yap: Set of 4 DVDs
Informative and entertaining, classical Feng Shui comes alive in *Discover Feng Shui with Joey Yap!*

You have the questions. Now let Joey personally answer them in this 4-set DVD compilation! Learn how to ensure the viability of your residence or workplace, Feng Shui-wise, without having to convert it into a Chinese antiques' shop. Classical Feng Shui is about harnessing the natural power of your environment to improve quality of life. It's a systematic and subtle metaphysical science.

Walking the Dragons with Joey Yap (The TV Series)

This DVD set features eight episodes, covering various landform Feng Shui analyses and applications from Joey Yap as he and his co-hosts travel through China. It includes case studies of both modern and historical sites with a focus on Yin House (burial places) Feng Shui and the tombs of the Qing Dynasty emperors.

The series was partly filmed on-location in mainland China, and the state of Selangor, Malaysia.

Mini Feng Shui Compass

The Mini Feng Shui Compass is a self-aligning compass that is not only light at 100gms but also built sturdily to ensure it will be convenient to use anywhere. The rings on the Mini Feng Shui Compass are bi-lingual and incorporate the 24 Mountain Rings that is used in your traditional Luo Pan.

The comprehensive booklet included will guide you in applying the 24 Mountain Directions on your Mini Feng Shui Compass effectively and the 8 Mansions Feng Shui to locate the most auspicious locations within your home, office and surroundings. You can also use the Mini Feng Shui Compass when measuring the direction of your property for the purpose of applying Flying Stars Feng Shui.

www.masteryacademy.com | +603 - 2284 8080

Online Home Study Courses

Gain Valuable Knowledge from the Comfort of Your Home

Now, armed with your trusty computer or laptop and Internet access, knowledge of Chinese Metaphysics is just a click away!

3 easy steps to activate your Home Study Course:

Step 1:
Go to the URL as indicated on the Activation Card, and key in your Activation Code

Step 2:
At the Registration page, fill in the details accordingly to enable us to generate your Student Identification (Student ID).

Step 3:
Upon successful registration, you may begin your lessons immediately.

Joey Yap's Feng Shui Mastery HomeStudy Course

Module 1: Empowering Your Home
Module 2: Master Practitioner Program

Learn how easy it is to harness the power of the environment to promote health, wealth and prosperity in your life. The knowledge and applications of Feng Shui will no more be a mystery but a valuable tool you can master on your own.

Joey Yap's BaZi Mastery HomeStudy Course

Module 1: Mapping Your Life
Module 2: Mastering Your Future

Discover your path of least resistance to success with insights about your personality and capabilities, and what strengths you can tap on to maximize your potential for success and happiness by mastering BaZi (Chinese Astrology). This course will teach you all the essentials you need to interpret a BaZi chart and more.

Joey Yap's Mian Xiang Mastery HomeStudy Course

Module 1: Face Reading
Module 2: Advanced Face Reading

A face can reveal so much about a person. Now, you can learn the art and science of Mian Xiang (Chinese Face Reading) to understand a person's character based on his or her facial features with ease and confidence.

www.masteryacademy.com | +603 - 2284 8080

Feng Shui Mastery™
LIVE COURSES (MODULES ONE TO FOUR)

An ideal program for those who wants to achieve mastery in Feng Shui from the comfort of their home. This comprehensive program covers the foundation up to the advanced practitioner levels, touching upon the important theories from various classical Feng Shui systems including Ba Zhai, San Yuan, San He and Xuan Kong.

Module One: Beginners Course

Module Two: Practitioners Course

Module Three: Advanced Practitioners Course

Module Four: Master Course

BaZi Mastery™
LIVE COURSES (MODULES ONE TO FOUR)

This lesson-based program brings a thorough introduction to BaZi and guides the student step-by-step all the way to the professional practitioner level. From the theories to the practical, BaZi students – along with serious Feng Shui practitioners – can master its application with accuracy and confidence.

Module One: Intensive Foundation Course

Module Two: Practitioners Course

Module Three: Advanced Practitioners Course

Module Four: Master Course in BaZi

Xuan Kong Mastery™
LIVE COURSES (MODULES ONE TO THREE)
Advanced Courses For Master Practitioners

Xuan Kong is a sophisticated branch of Feng Shui, replete with many techniques and formulae, which encompass numerology, symbology and the science of the Ba Gua, along with the mathematics of time. This program is ideal for practitioners looking to bring their practice to a more in-depth level.

Module One: Advanced Foundation Course

Module Two A: Advanced Xuan Kong Methodologies

Module Two B: Purple White

Module Three: Advanced Xuan Kong Da Gua

www.masteryacademy.com | +603 - 2284 8080

Mian Xiang Mastery™
LIVE COURSES (MODULES ONE AND TWO)

This program comprises of two modules, each carefully developed to allow students to familiarize with the fundamentals of Mian Xiang or Face Reading and the intricacies of its theories and principles. With lessons guided by video lectures, slide presentations and notes, students are able to understand and practice Mian Xiang with greater depth.

Module One: Basic Face Reading

Module Two: Practical Face Reading

Yi Jing Mastery™
LIVE COURSES (MODULES ONE AND TWO)

Whether you're a casual or serious Yi Jing enthusiast, this lesson-based program contains two modules that brings students deeper into the Chinese science of divination. The lessons will guide students on the mastery of its sophisticated formulas and calculations to derive answers to questions we pose.

Module One: Traditional Yi Jing

Module Two: Plum Blossom Numerology

Ze Ri Mastery™
LIVE COURSES (MODULES ONE AND TWO)

In two modules, students will undergo a thorough instruction on the fundamentals of ZeRi or Date Selection. The comprehensive program covers Date Selection for both Personal and Feng Shui purposes to Xuan Kong Da Gua Date Selection.

Module One: Personal and Feng Shui Date Selection

Module Two: Xuan Kong Da Gua Date Selection

www.masteryacademy.com | +603 - 2284 8080

Feng Shui for Life

This is an entry-level five-day course designed for the Feng Shui beginner to learn the application of practical Feng Shui in day-to-day living. Lessons include quick tips on analyzing the BaZi chart, simple Feng Shui solutions for the home, basic Date Selection, useful Face Reading techniques and practical Water formulas. A great introduction course on Chinese Metaphysics studies for beginners.

Joey Yap's Design Your Destiny

This is a three-day life transformation program designed to inspire awareness and action for you to create a better quality of life. It introduces the DRT™ (Decision Referential Technology) method, which utilizes the BaZi Personality Profiling system to determine the right version of you, and serves as a tool to help you make better decisions and achieve a better life in the least resistant way possible based on your Personality Profile Type.

Walk the Mountains! Learn Feng Shui in a Practical and Hands-on Program

Feng Shui Mastery Excursion™

Learn landform (Luan Tou) Feng Shui by walking the mountains and chasing the Dragon's vein in China. This Program takes the students in a study tour to examine notable Feng Shui landmarks, mountains, hills, valleys, ancient palaces, famous mansions, houses and tombs in China. The Excursion is a 'practical' hands-on course where students are shown to perform readings using the formulas they've learnt and to recognize and read Feng Shui Landform (Luan Tou) formations.

Read about China Excursion here:
http://www.fengshuiexcursion.com

Mastery Academy courses are conducted around the world. Find out when will Joey Yap be in your area by visiting **www.masteryacademy.com** or call our office at **+603-2284 8080**.

---

www.masteryacademy.com | +603 - 2284 8080